MW01711543

The Biographical Dictionary Game

BLUFFLE

No pieces to lose!

No unnecessary board!

Easy to store and find!

No complicated rules!

More than 1000 names!

Carolynne Veffer ★ Wendy Thomas

GAMEBOOKS

TORONTO

Note: The above disclaimer does not apply to the perforated answer sheets at the back of the book. Readers are invited to photocopy them as needed.

GameBooks, Box 240, 2255-B Queen Street East,

Toronto, Ontario, M4E 1G5

Design by Molly Brass

Printed and bound in Canada by Best Gagné Printing

ISBN: 0-9698240-0-9

Thanks to everyone who helped in our research by providing names, information, and encouragement and to the people who have lived in obscurity until now...

Bluffle *v.* **1** To deceive your opponents by inventing the most convincing claim to fame. **2** To have hours of fun with friends and/or family at home, at the cottage, on a boat, on a train. **3** To learn who invented Silly Putty; who designed the unsinkable *Titanic*; who was the first airline stewardess. *n.* **1** A book that is an entertaining game. **2** A book that is source of fascinating information.

Blufflebag *n.* Any bag in which you can carry this book, some paper, and a few pens or pencils.

Bluffleboard *n.* Any board game with a start and finish point that can be used as an alternative for scoring in Bluffle.

INTRODUCTION

Contained in these pages is an eclectic collection of over a thousand names to use in this new variation of bluffing games such as Balderdash, Slang Teasers, and the Dictionary Game.

The people in this book have done interesting, unusual, wacky, important, and – often – forgotten things. As much as possible, we chose names that were unusual in themselves.

Some names may be known to particular groups of people – for example, teachers may recognize the name of the person who started the kindergarten system, computer experts may recognize the name of the people who invented BASIC. So, as you flip through the pages to select a name, you can use your knowledge of the interests, careers, and experiences of the other players to choose a name they are unlikely to know.

We have attempted to verify all names in at least two sources, but please let us know if you think you've found an error.

PLAYING THE GAME

Object of the game:
To bluff the other players by making up the most convincing claim to fame

Number of players:
Most successful with four or more

Materials:
Pens or pencils and a sheet of paper for scoring.
The rest is in the book!
(Answer sheets are included at the back of the book. Keep one as a master to photocopy more.)

1 One player (the Biographer) chooses a name, reads the name aloud, and spells it if necessary.

2 Each player invents a short claim to fame for that person and writes it on the Answer Sheet.

3 The Biographer writes the true claim to fame – printed in bold – on an Answer Sheet. *(See Hints)*

4 Players hand the completed and initialled Answer Sheets to the Biographer.

5 The Biographer reads each one aloud in random order, including the true one.

6 Players vote for the most convincing claim to fame. The Biographer records on the Answer Sheets the number of votes each gets.

7 The next player becomes the Biographer and play continues. Players can agree at the start of the game what constitutes the end.

Scoring:

★ One point is awarded for each vote your bluff gets

★ One point is awarded when you vote for the true claim to fame

★ One point is awarded to the Biographer if no one chooses the true claim to fame

★★ Two points are awarded for knowing the true claim to fame *(see Hints)*

HINTS

***Q.* What is the purpose of the additional information?**
A. To make the Biographer's job more creative, he or she can choose to incorporate additional facts in the true claim to fame.

***Q.* What if I know the true claim to fame of the person?**
A. Write it down and hand it to the Biographer, saying that you know the correct answer. The Biographer sets it aside after ensuring that it is the correct answer. You automatically get two points and do not vote in that round. If your answer is not the same as that provided in Bluffle, the Biographer will return your sheet and ask you to provide another claim to fame.

***Q.* Can I vote for my own answer to fool the others?**
A. Yes, but you do not receive a point for your vote.

***Q.* Can the Biographer take part in any other way?**
A. The Biographer can choose to make up an additional claim to fame to include with the others.

***Q.* What if I prefer to play with a board and pieces?**
A. We've kept Bluffle simple, but you can keep score using any board that has a start and finish.

***Q.* What about other questions not covered by "playing the game"?**
A. Work out solutions to contentious issues not covered here. Remember – it's only a game!

LEE
AAKER 1952-

★ **He played Rusty in the TV series " Rin Tin Tin."**

CLEVELAND
ABBE 1838-1916

★ **Initiated daily weather bulletins; in 1869.**
★ American meteorologist; also pioneered standard time in U.S.

RUDOLF
ABEL 1903-1971

★ **Russian spy exchanged for Francis Gary Powers in 1962.**
★ Powers was a U-2 pilot shot down over the Soviet Union. Abel had been convicted of spying in the United States.

JEAN
ACKER 1893-1978

★ **Her 1919 marriage to Rudolph Valentino lasted less than six hours; she locked him out on their wedding night.**

CASWELL
ADAMS 1907-1957

★ **American sportswriter who coined the term Ivy League.**
★ Term describes U.S. colleges and universities; now indicates prestige and excellence but he used it in a disparaging way.

WILLIAM
ADAMS 1564-1620

★ **The first Englishman to visit Japan; in 1600.**
★ American author James Clavell used Adams as the prototype for the character "Blackthorn" in his 1975 novel *Shogun*.

LUCIE ADELSBERGER 1896-1971

★ **German-born American medical researcher who discovered that changes in red blood cells were a warning of cancer.**

CLÉMENT ADER 1841-1925

★ **German inventor who patented first stereo system; in 1881.**

★ Also invented a stereophonic telephone system and patented a V-8 motor car engine and air-cushion hydrofoil.

RICHARD ADLER 1921-

★ **He wrote the music and lyrics for "Damn Yankees" and "Pajama Game."**

★ His collaborator was Jerry Ross (1926-1955).

ROBERT AITKEN 1734-1802

★ **Published the first complete English Bible printed in the United States; in 1782.**

P.F.F. ALBEE

★ **She was the first Avon Lady.**

WALTER ALCOCK

★ **Englishman who invented the perforated toilet paper roll in 1879.**

ERNST FREDERIK WERNER ALEXANDERSON 1878-1975

★ **Invented the first home television in 1927.**

★ Also responsible for the device that made voice communication possible. In all, he held over 200 patents in radio and television.

ALEXANDER VASSILIEVICH ALEXANDROV 1883-1946

★ **Composer of the Soviet national anthem.**

★ Words were by S. Mikhalkov. Became the anthem in 1943.

THOMAS CLIFFORD ALLBUTT 1836-1925

★ **He introduced the short clinic thermometer; in 1866.**

★ Thermometers had been a foot long and had to be kept in place for 20 minutes.

EUPHEMIA ALLEN

★ **Credited with writing piano exercise "Chopsticks" in 1877.**

★ She wrote it under the pseudonym Arthur de Lulli. The original title was "The Celebrated Chop Waltz."

ROGER ERNEST COLLINGWOOD ALTOUNYAN 1922-1987

★ **Inventor of the asthma inhaler and the drug Intal.**

★ He suffered from asthma himself.

KIRK ALYN 1910-

★ **First actor to play Superman in the movies, in the 1940s.**

A

JACOB
AMMAN c.1645-c.1730

★ **Leader of the group that established the Amish.**
★ The "breakaway" Swiss Mennonites were named after Amman.

OTHMAR HERMANN
AMMANN 1897-1965

★ **American engineer who designed the Golden Gate Bridge in 1935 and the Verrazano-Narrows Bridge in 1964.**

DANIEL
AMMEN 1819-1898

★ **Responsible for bringing goldfish to the United States from Japan; in 1878. It started the goldfish craze.**

LALE
ANDERSEN 1911-1972

★ **German singer of the World War II song "Lili Marlene."**
★ Her real name was Liselotte Helen Beul.

LEW
ANDERSON

★ **Last man to play Clarabell on "Howdy Doody."**

SWAN FRITEAF
ANDERSON 1879-1963

★ **He developed the machine for making Eskimo Pies.**

JOHN
ANDRÉ 1751-1780

★ **He was Benedict Arnold's co-conspirator.**

SALOMON AUGUST ANDRÉE 1854-1897

★ **He died trying to fly over the north pole in a balloon.**

CHRISTOPHER HOWARD ANDREWES 1896-1988

★ **Helped discover the common cold virus.**

LANCELOT ANDREWES 1555-1626

★ **Helped produce the King James version of the Bible; in 1607.**

STANLEY ANDREWS 1892-1969

★ **The first host of "Death Valley Days."**

★ He was replaced by Ronald Reagan.

JIMMY ANGEL 1899-1956

★ **Discovered Angel Falls in Venezuela; in 1929.**

★ Angel Falls is the world's highest waterfall.

MARY ANNING 1799-1847

★ **Discovered first fossil remains of a pterodactyl.**

★ She found her first fossil, an ichthysaurus, in 1811 at the age of 12.

FRANCESCO ANTOMMARCHI 1780-1838

★ **Napoleon's physician while he was on St. Helena from 1818 until Napoleon's death in 1821.**

VIRGINIA
APGAR

1909-1974

★ **American doctor who developed the Apgar Score, a test that quickly determines the health of a newborn baby.**

★ The test is given within a minute of the baby's birth. It checks the heart rate, respiration, muscle tone, reflexes, and colour.

CHARLES NICOLAS
APPERT

1750-1841

★ **The first to preserve food in sealed containers; in 1795.**

★ He applied heat for sterilization, first to bottles (in 1809) then to cans (in 1815).

STANLEY
APPLEBAUM

1933-

★ **Real name of singer and actor Robert Goulet.**

CONSTANCE M.K.
APPLEBEE

★ **Introduced women's field hockey to the United States.**

★ First played at Vassar College in1901.

WILLIAM
ARKWRIGHT

1857-1925

★ **D.H. Lawrence based Sir Clifford Chatterley on him.**

★ He was unhappily married to Agnes Mary Summers-Cox.

SALVINO DEGLI
ARMATI

1245-1317

★ **Invented the magnifying glass; in the 13th century.**

★ He is also credited with inventing eyeglasses.

ARCHIBALD
ARMSTRONG D.1672

★ **He was the court-jester to James I and Charles I.**

EDWIN HOWARD
ARMSTRONG 1890-1954

★ **American radio engineer who invented FM radio in 1933.**
★ There were long battles over the invention. Armstrong, regarded as Edison's equal, committed suicide in midst of lawsuits over the patents of his many ingenious inventions.

THOMAS AUGUSTINE
ARNE 1710-1778

★ **English composer who wrote "Rule, Britannia" in 1740.**

JOSEPH
ARNOLD 1782-1818

★ **English botanist who discovered the largest flower in the world.**
★ It was one yard across and weighed 15 pounds.

SVANTE AUGUST
ARRHENIUS 1859-1927

★ **Swedish scientist who discovered the "greenhouse effect" of carbon dioxide in 1896.**

MANUEL
ARTIME 1932-1977

★ **Cuban exile who led the 1961 Bay of Pigs invasion of Cuba.**

DOROTHY
ARZNER 1900-1979

★ **First female director of Hollywood talkies.**

★ In 1929 directed Paramount's first sound film. Also said to be first to use an overhead microphone, dangling it from a fishing pole.

GEORGE
ASAF 1880-1951

★ **He wrote the words to "Pack Up Your Troubles in Your Old Kit-Bag"; in 1915.**

★ The music was written by Felix Powell.

WILLIAM
ASHER 1919-

★ **Director of the Beach Party movies: Beach Party, Bikini Beach, Beach Blanket Bingo, and How to Stuff a Wild Bikini.**

★ He is also the husband of actress Elizabeth Montgomery and was the producer of "Bewitched."

EMMETT LITTLETON
ASHFORD 1915-1980

★ **First black umpire in major league baseball.**

JOSEPH
ASPDIN 1779-1855

★ **Patented Portland cement in 1824.**

EDWARD
ASSELBERGS

★ **Invented instant mashed potato flakes in 1961.**

★ Canadian doctor working with a team at Agriculture Canada attempting to develop many other instant products.

JOHN P. ATHERTON

★ **He wrote the song for the catchy Brylcreem commercial "Brylcreem, a Little Dab'll Do Ya"; in 1949.**

CRISPUS ATTUCKS c.1723-1779

★ **First casualty of the American Revolution.**

★ He was a runaway slave who became leader of the group protesting taxes. He was the first of five people who died in the Boston Massacre.

AW BOON-HAW 1883-1954

★ **Made his fortune from the patent medicine Tiger Balm.**

★ Hong Kong businessman; head of the Sing Tao newspaper group.

GLADYS AYLWARD 1903-1970

★ **Her life was depicted in the movie "Inn of the Sixth Happiness."**

★ British missionary portrayed in the film by Ingrid Bergman.

★ She led 100 homeless children out of the war zone to safety during the Japanese invasion of China.

DIANA AYOUB

★ **Paul Anka's babysitter who is the Diana in his hit song.**

NNAMDI AZIKIWE 1904-

★ **First president of independent Nigeria; from 1963 to 1966.**

ART BABBIT / DICK HEUMER

★ **Cartoonists who originally drew Donald Duck.**

STEPHEN MOULTON BABCOCK 1843-1931

★ **American chemist who invented the process to determine the butter fat content of milk; in 1890.**

FRANK GERARD BACK

★ **He invented the zoom lens in 1945.**

HENRY BACON 1866-1924

★ **Designed the Lincoln Memorial; in 1922.**

LEO HENDRIK BAEKELAND 1863-1944

★ **Invented the first completely synthetic material, the plastic Bakelite; in 1909.**

★ Belgian-born U.S. chemist; founder of the Bakelite Corporation in 1910; now part of Union Carbide.

ROSS BAGDASARIAN 1919-1972

★ **Creator and voices of Alvin and the Chipmunks.**

JAMES ANTHONY BAILEY 1847-1906

★ **The Bailey half of Barnum and Bailey Circus.**

JOHN LOGIE BAIRD 1888-1946

★ **In 1925 he transmitted a TV picture.**

★ He is one of several inventors credited with inventing TV; also pioneered fibre optics and transmitted colour TV in 1939.

BERNT BALCHEN 1899-1973

★ **U.S. aviator who piloted Richard Byrd on the first flight over the South Pole in 1929.**

FRED BALDASARE

★ **American who was the first to swim the English Channel underwater; in 1962.**

★ He used scuba equipment to perform the feat.

FREDERICK WALKER "CASEY" BALDWIN 1882-1948

★ **First Canadian to fly an airplane; on March 12, 1908**

★ He was the seventh person in the world to fly.

CORNELIUS "NEAL" BALL 1881-1957

★ **First major league baseball player to make an unassisted triple play; on July 19, 1909.**

ERNEST R. BALL 1878-1927

★ **Wrote "When Irish Eyes Are Smiling"; in 1912.**

★ The lyrics were written by Chauncey Olcott and George Graff, Jr.

★ Although he wrote other "Irish" ballads, he was born in Ohio.

HANK
BALLARD

★ **Wrote the song "The Twist" in 1958.**
★ He saw teenagers doing a dance, lifting each foot off the floor, swinging their arms, sticking their bottoms out and shaking them.

DON CAMERON
BALLOONS

★ **Built the largest functional Christmas cracker — 108.5 feet long — in 1988.**

SIRIMAVO RATWATTE DIAS
BANDARANAIKE 1916-

★ **First woman in the world to be elected prime minister.**
★ Prime minister of Ceylon (Sri Lanka), 1960 to 1965, 1970 to 1977. Her husband was prime minister until his assassination in 1959.

FRANK
BANK

★ **Played Clarence "Lumpy" Rutherford on "Leave It To Beaver."**

DAN
BANKHEAD 1920-1976

★ **First black pitcher in major league baseball; in 1947.**
★ He played for the Brooklyn Dodgers.

DANIEL
BARBARO 1513-1570

★ **Built the first plant conservatory; in 1545.**
★ It was located in the botanical gardens in Pavia, Italy, and was heated in winter by a brazier or open hearth.

SABINE BARING-GOULD 1834-1924

★ **Wrote the words to "Onward Christian Soldiers"; in 1871.**

★ English clergyman; the music was written by Sir Arthur Sullivan.

FLORENCE LOW BARNES 1902-1975

★ **First woman stunt pilot in motion pictures.**

JANE BARRY 1795-1865

★ **The first woman doctor; in 1812.**

★ Masqueraded as Dr. James Barry; had affairs and an illegitimate child, but her sex was not officially acknowledged until she died.

JACOB BARSIMON

★ **He was the first American Jew.**

★ He arrived in New Amsterdam on August 22, 1654. A month later, 23 Dutch Jewish refugees from the Brazilian inquisition arrived.

FRÉDÉRIC AUGUSTE BARTHOLDI 1834-1904

★ **Designer of the Statue of Liberty.**

★ He used his mother, Charlotte Beysser Bartholdi, as the model.

ROBERT ABRAM BARTLETT 1875-1946

★ **Canadian commander of the ship that took Robert Peary on his first attempt to reach the North Pole.**

★ Also accompanied Peary on his last trip to the pole (1908-1909).

EDMUND
BARTON 1849-1920

★ **First prime minister of Australia; from 1901 to 1903.**

GIAMBATTISTA
BASILE 1575-1632

★ **Wrote the first version of "Sleeping Beauty" in 1636.**

KATHERINE LEE
BATES 1859-1929

★ **Author of the words for "America the Beautiful."**

★ Her inspiration came climbing Pike's Peak. Words were printed in 1895 and set to the music of Samuel A. Ward's "Materna."

HILMAR R.
BAUKHAGE 1889-1976

★ **First to read the national nightly TV news; in 1948 on ABC.**

JOSEPHINE HOLT
BAY 1900-

★ **She was the first woman to head a member firm of the New York Stock Exchange.**

THOMAS FRANCIS
BAYARD 1828-1898

★ **Was the first U.S. ambassador to Britain; from 1893 to 1897.**

ALFRED E.
BEACH

★ **Built the first subway system in New York in 1870.**

★ It was 296 feet long; its cars were propelled by compressed air.

CLARENCE H. "GINGER" BEAUMONT 1876-1956

★ **The first man to bat in a World Series game (1903).**

★ Played for Pittsburgh. It was between Boston and Pittsburgh. Boston took the series 5-3 but Pittsburgh won the first game 7-3.

HUGH (SIR) BEAVER 1890-1967

★ **Had the idea for the *Guinness Book of Records*.**

★ After debates about which game bird was the fastest, Sir Hugh, director of the Guinness brewery, realized this kind of argument arose in pubs daily. He employed a fact and figure agency to compile a book of records. In1955, the first book was printed.

BRACE BELL BEEMER 1903-1965

★ **Was the voice of the Lone Ranger on radio from 1941 to 1954.**

WILLIAM GEORGE BEERS 1841-1900

★ **Dentist who standardized the rules for lacrosse; in 1860.**

★ The game was first played by the Algonquian Indians and is the oldest organized sport in North America.

SOSTHENES BEHN 1882-1957

★ **Founder, president and chairman of the board of ITT.**

★ His reign extended from 1920 to1956.

PAUL BEIERSDORF

★ **German pharmacist who invented Nivea cream; in 1911.**

DEBENNEVILLE "BERT" BELL 1895-1959

★ **NFL commissioner who instituted the TV blackout rule.**

★ He also suggested in 1935 the college draft system to balance teams so the richest teams wouldn't always get the best players.

JOSEPH BELL 1837-1911

★ **Sir Arthur Conan Doyle acknowledged that this professor and surgeon was the inspiration for Sherlock Holmes.**

EDWARD BELLAMY 1850-1898

★ **He coined the term "credit card"; in 1888.**

★ He believed that by 2000, each U.S. citizen would carry a card indicating his/her share of the "annual product of the nation."

FRANCIS M. BELLAMY

★ **Wrote U.S. Pledge of Allegiance; in 1892.**

★ He wrote it to commemorate Columbus Day in public schools.

GIOVANNI BATTISTA BELZONI 1778-1823

★ **Italian archaeologist who opened the temple of Abu Simbel.**

★ Discovered the tomb of Seti I; opened the second pyramid at Giza.

FRANÇOIS JOSEPH BELZUNG

★ **French engineer who patented screw-top bottles; in 1852.**

JAMES GORDON
BENNETT 1841-1918

★ **He was the editor of the *New York Herald* who sent Stanley to Africa to find Livingstone in 1869.**

ARTHUR CHRISTOPHER
BENSON 1862-1925

★ **Wrote the lyrics for "Land of Hope and Glory."**

★ The music was by Elgar (Opus 39, No.1).

EMILE
BERLINER 1851-1929

★ **Was granted a patent for the gramophone; in 1887.**

★ Also invented the flat "platter" phonograph record (replacing the cylindrical disc) in 1877; improved telephone and airplane motors; leading advocate for compulsory pasteurization of milk.

JOHN JERVIS
BARNARD D.1954

★ **Originated the British soccer pool betting system in 1921.**

MICHELINE
BARNARDI

★ **Modelled the first bikini; in 1946.**

★ She was a dancer in Paris. Professional models initially refused to wear the bikini.

WILLIAM
BERNBACH 1911-1982

★ **Advertising executive who created the popular character Juan Valdez for Colombian coffee.**

★ Also Avis slogan "When you're number two, you try harder."

ROSE
BERTIN
1747-1813

★ **Marie Antoinette's dressmaker.**

JOHN JACOB "JAY"
BERWANGER
1914-

★ **First winner of the Heisman trophy; in 1935.**
★ Also the first chosen in first NFL draft of college players in 1936. The trophy is given to the best college player.

KRISHNA
BHANJI
1943-

★ **Real name of actor Ben Kingsley.**
★ He was born in Yorkshire, England.

KARNA RAM
BHEEL
1928-1987

★ **Grew a moustache that was 7 feet 10 inches from tip to tip.**

MARCEL
BICH
1914-

★ **Founder, president and chairman of the board of BIC Pen Corporation.**

JAMES
BICKET

★ **Published the first book on curling in Canada; in 1840.**

FRANCIS BEVERLEY
BIDDLE
1886-1968

★ **He was the U.S. judge at the Nuremberg trials.**

ROWLAND HARRY
BIFFEN 1874-1949

★ **Established plant breeding as a science.**

IRA
BIFFLE

★ **Aviator who taught Charles Lindbergh to fly.**

EARL DERR
BIGGERS 1884-1933

★ **Writer who created Charlie Chan.**
★ His first book was *House without a Key*, published in 1925

JOHN MICHAEL WARD
BINGHAM 1908-

★ **le Carré's model for George Smiley.**
★ He was a thriller writer as well as an intelligence worker. John le Carré described him as "the most forgettable man I ever met."

NATHAN
BIRNBAUM 1896-

★ **Real name of George Burns.**

EMILY PERKINS
BISSELL 1861-1948

★ **She headed the first U.S. Christmas seal drive held in 1907.**

GEORGE WILLIAM
BITZER 1872-1944

★ **Cameraman on D.W. Griffith's "Birth of a Nation."**
★ He also developed closeups and long shots.

VILHELM FIRMAN KOREN
BJERKNES 1862-1951

★ **Developed the theory of weather fronts.**
★ Norwegian physicist; known as the father of meteorology.

LENA
BLACKBURNE

★ **Created Lena Blackburne Baseball Rubbing Mud; it's rubbed on baseballs before major league games to take the shine off.**

JAMES STEWART
BLACKTON 1875-1941

★ **In 1906 he produced the first animated cartoon.**
★ Called "Humorous Phases of Funny Faces"; aided by Emile Cohl.

ANTOINETTE LOUISA
BLACKWELL 1825-1909

★ **First ordained woman minister in the United States; in 1853.**
★ In the Congregational church; it became the Unitarian church.

ALFRED
BLALOCK 1899-1964

★ **The doctor who performed the first operation shown on closed-circuit TV; in 1947.**

PIERRE-LOUIS
BLANCARD

★ **French florist who brought the first chrysanthemums from China to France; in 1789.**
★ Chrysanthemums had made the trip before, but these were the first to survive.

JAMES A.
BLAND 1854-1911

★ **Wrote "Carry Me Back to Old Virginny"; in 1828.**
★ It was adopted as the Virginia state song; he also wrote "O Dem Golden Slippers."

CLARA
BLANDICK 1880-1962

★ **Actress who played Auntie Em in "The Wizard of Oz."**
★ She also played Aunt Polly in "Tom Sawyer" in 1930.

TOM
BLANKENSHIP

★ **Mark Twain based Huckleberry Finn on him.**
★ In real life he was the son of the local drunk in Hannibal, Missouri.

FRANCINA "FANNY" ELSJE
BLANKERS-KOEN 1918-

★ **She was the first woman to win four gold medals in one Olympics; in 1948.**
★ She was a 30-year-old Dutch mother of two when she won her medals in track and field in London.

GEORGE C.
BLICKENSDERFER 1850-1917

★ **Invented the portable typewriter; in 1892.**

HENRY H.
BLISS 1828-1899

★ **First American to die as a result of a car accident; in 1899.**
★ He was knocked down while getting off a New York streetcar.

SUSAN ELIZABETH
BLOW 1843-1916

★ **Opened first U.S. public kindergarten; in St. Louis in 1873.**

MERWYN A.
BOGUE 1908-

★ **Real name of Ish Kabibble.**
★ He was a singer/comic with Kay Kyser's band.

CHARLES "BUDDY"
BOLDEN 1868-1931

★ **Formed the first jazz band in the United States; in 1895.**

TERRY JEAN
BOLLETTE 1953-

★ **Real name of Hulk Hogan.**
★ His vital statistics: 6 feet, 8 inches, 300 pounds.

BERTRAM BORDEN
BOLTWOOD 1870-1927

★ **Developed the method of uranium dating of rock.**

MARGARET GRACE
BONDFIELD 1873-1953

★ **First female to be a British cabinet minister.**
★ She was the Minister of Labour from 1929 to 1931.

HUBERT CECIL
BOOTH 1872-1955

★ **In 1901 he patented the first vacuum cleaner.**
★ It needed two people to use it. It was used to vacuum the carpet in Westminster Abbey for Edward VII's coronation.

OLIVER BOOTH

★ **He started the sport of ice sailing when he fitted a sailboat with blades; in 1790.**

★ The boat consisted of a square box on three iron-covered runners, a sail, a rudder post, and wooden tiller.

JOHN GUTZON BORGLUM 1867-1941

★ **Designed and carved the figures on Mt. Rushmore.**

★ It cost the U.S. government $1 million; took from 1929-1941 to complete; son Lincoln continued after his father's death.

PIERRE MARCELLIN BOULE 1870-1942

★ **French paleontologist who was the first to construct a complete Neanderthal skeleton; in 1908.**

MARCEL BOULESTIN 1878-1943

★ **He became the first television cook in 1937.**

★ French chef who appeared on the BBC program "Cook's Night Out." The first program demonstrated how to make an omelette.

ELIZABETH ANGELA MARGUERITE BOWES-LYON 1900-

★ **The Queen Mum.**

LOUISE ARNER BOYD 1887-1972

★ **First woman to make a successful flight over and around the North Pole; in 1955.**

ANNE
BRADSTREET c.1612-1672

★ **Wrote the first book of poems in the United States; in 1650.**
★ Book was called *The Tenth Muse Lately Sprung Up in America.* The poems were first published in England without her knowledge.

JACQUES EDWIN
BRANDENBERGER 1872-1954

★ **Swiss chemist who invented cellophane; in 1912.**
★ The creation of cellophane led to the development of nylon.

HUGH "LUMPY"
BRANNUM

★ **He portrayed Mr. Green Jeans on "Captain Kangaroo."**

CHRISTOPHER
BRASHER

CHRISTOPHER
CHATAWAY

★ **They were Roger Bannister's pacemakers when Bannister ran the first 4-minute mile; in 1954.**

NORMAN
BREAKEY

★ **Canadian who invented the paint roller; in 1940.**
★ He couldn't afford to patent it and died without benefiting from the financial success of his invention.

NICHOLAS
BREAKSPEAR 1100-1159

★ **The only English pope.**
★ He was Pope Adrian IV from 1154-1159.

HARRY
BREARLEY 1871-1948

★ **First to cast stainless steel; in Sheffield, England, in 1913.**

★ Others accomplished the same that year — Elwood Haynes in the United States and Edward Maurer and Benno Strauss in Germany.

VICTOR DAVID
BRENNER 1871-1924

★ **Sculptor who designed the Lincoln cent, issued in 1909.**

★ It was the first coin bearing the portrait of a president.

LAURA DEWEY
BRIDGMAN 1829-1889

★ **First deaf and blind child educated in the United States.**

★ She preceded Helen Keller and was educated by Dr. Samuel Howe at the Perkins Instiute.

ABRAHAM ARDEN
BRILL 1875-1948

★ **Was the first to translate the works of Freud into English.**

★ Austrian-born U.S. psychiatrist who also translated Jung.

JOHN
BROADWOOD 1732-1012

★ **He patented the piano pedals for the pianoforte in 1783.**

WILLIAM
BRODIE 1741-1788

★ **The robber on whom Dr. Jekyll and Mr. Hyde is based.**

★ Scottish cabinetmaker and robber.

LEV DAYDOVICH
BRONSTEIN 1879-1940

★ **Real name of Leon Trotsky.**

FRANCES MOORE
BROOKE 1745-1789

★ **First novelist in Canada.**
★ The book was *The History of Emily Montague*, published in 1769.

NORMAN EVERARD
BROOKES 1877-1968

★ **First lefty to win a Wimbledon championship; in 1907.**
★ Australian tennis player who was also the first overseas player to win men's singles at Wimbledon.

CHARLES
BROOKS, JR. D.1982

★ **First prisoner executed in the U.S. by lethal injection; in 1982.**

JOHN "JACK"
BROUGHTON 1705-1789

★ **In 1747, invented the first boxing gloves, called mufflers.**
★ English fighter who also drew up the first rules of barefisted boxing in 1743.

RICOU
BROWNING 1930-

★ **Stuntman who played the title role in "The Creature from the Black Lagoon" in the underwater scenes; in 1954.**
★ Ben Chapman played the monster above water.
★ Browning also wrote the original story for "Flipper."

WILLIAM
BROWNRIGG 1711-1800

★ **Invented carbonated mineral water in 1741 (in Great Britain).**

SPANGLER ARLINGTON
BRUGH 1911-

★ **Real name of actor Robert Taylor.**

ALYS McKEY
BRYANT

★ **The first woman to fly a plane in Canada; in 1913.**

PHILIPPE
BUACHE 1700-?

★ **Geographer who devised contour lines for maps and charts.**

EDWIN
BUDDING

★ **Invented and patented the first manual lawn mower; in 1831.**

MORGAN GARDENER
BULKELEY 1837-1922

★ **First president of the National Baseball League.**
★ Served only one year, in 1876.

EPHRAIM WALES
BULL 1806-1895

★ **American horticulturist who developed the Concord grape.**
★ The grape was first exhibited in 1853.

WILLIAM CHRISTIAN

BULLITT 1891-1967

★ **First U.S. ambassador to the U.S.S.R.; from 1933 to 1936.**
★ After that, he was ambassador to France from 1936 to 1941.

WALTER HENRY

BULPITT

★ **Invented the safety switch for electric kettles in 1931.**

CHARLES

BUNBURY

★ **Owner of the first horse (Diomed) to win the Derby; in 1780.**
★ The purse was the equivalent of $5,620.

MAY GODFRAY SUTTON

BUNDY 1886-1975

★ **First U.S. woman to win singles title at Wimbledon; in 1905.**
★ Also first to win Wimbledon in debut performance.
★ In the 1930 U.S. Women's Open, she slipped and fractured her left leg. She got hold of a crutch and finished playing.

GEORGE

BUNTING 1870-1959

★ **Baltimore pharmacist who invented Noxzema; in 1914.**
★ Originally Dr. Bunting's Sunburn Remedy, sold in small blue jars.

FRANK GELETT

BURGESS 1866-1951

★ **The American humorist who coined the word blurb; in 1907.**
★ The name came from a sexy character, Miss Belinda Blurb, used on a comic-book jacket that he had created.

FANNY
BURNEY 1751-1840

★ **First Englishwoman to write a novel.**
★ The first was called *Evelina* and was published in 1778.

BENJAMIN HAPGOOD
BURT

★ **He introduced the phrase "When you're all dressed up and no place to go" in his song of the same name; in 1913.**

NOLAND
BUSCHNEL 1944-

★ **Created the first commercial video game, Pong; in 1972.**
★ He was a 28-year-old American student when he started to build the Atari company from this game.

DOROTHY VREDENBURGH
BUSH 1916-1991

★ **The woman who read the state roll at the U.S. Democratic Conventions for 40 years (from 1948 to 1988).**

JOHN
BUSHELL 1715-1761

★ **Publisher of the oldest paper in Canada.**
★ It was the *Halifax Gazette*, first issued on March 23, 1752.

ADOLF FRIEDRICH JOHANN
BUTENANDT 1903-

★ **German chemist who synthesized testosterone.**
★ He also isolated estrone, androsterone, and progesterone.

MELVIN
CALVIN 1911-

★ **He discovered how the process of photosynthesis works.**

RUDOLF JAKOB
CAMERARIUS 1665-1721

★ **German botanist who discovered pollen in plants; in 1694.**

WALTER CHAUNCEY
CAMP 1859-1925

★ **Football innovator who established the scrimmage line, centre snap, downs and 11 players per side.**

MARTHA JANE
CANARY 1852-1903

★ **Real name of Calamity Jane.**

★ She worked as a teamster in U.S. mining camps, transporting supplies to camps. She adopted male dress and was an excellent shot, promising "calamity" to aggressors.

ANNIE JUMP
CANNON 1863-1941

★ **First woman to receive an honorary degree from Oxford; in 1925.**

★ American astronomer who discovered more than 300 variable stars and five novae.

JOSEPH GURNEY
CANNON 1836-1926

★ **American Congressman who was on the first cover of *Time* magazine; in 1923.**

JUAN SEBASTIAN
CANO

★ **He was the Portuguese discoverer of the mouth of the Congo River; in 1484.**

JOHN
CANTON 1718-1772

★ **English physicist who made the first artificial magnets.**

J.F.
CANTRELL

★ **Opened first laundromat; in 1934 in Fort Worth, Texas.**
★ He called it the Washeteria.

ENOS EDWARD "YAKIMA"
CANUTT 1895-1986

★ **The double for Clark Gable in "Gone with the Wind" and John Wayne in "Stagecoach."**
★ He was a rodeo champion and stuntman. He received a special Oscar in 1966 for special achievements as a stuntman.

TONY
CANZONERI 1908-1959

★ **Held the world light welterweight title for only 33 days, the shortest period for any boxer.**

KAREL MATELJ
CAPEK 1890-1938

★ **Czech playwright who coined the word robot; in 1921.**
★ The word was introduced in his play *R.U.R.* (Rossum's Universal Robots) and is from the Czech word *robota* (work).

HATTIE OPHELIA WYATT CARAWAY 1878-1950

★ **First woman elected to the U.S. Senate; in 1931.**

ALLISON CARGILL

★ **A Glasgow schoolgirl who was the first Girl Scout; in 1908.**
★ When denied membership in Boy Scouts, she formed her own troop, becoming the first Girl Scout.

BOGART CARLAW 1904-1979

★ **Created the "Umm, umm good" slogan for Campbell's soup.**

ALEXANDER CARLISLE

★ **Chief designer of the "unsinkable" *Titanic*.**

CHESTER FLOYD CARLSON 1906-1968

★ **Invented the Xerox photocopying process; in 1938.**

WALLACE HUME CAROTHERS 1896-1937

★ **American chemist who developed nylon; in 1937.**
★ He committed suicide two months after patenting his invention and had no idea of its success.

JOHN GARNET CARTER 1883-1954

★ **Originator of miniature golf; in 1927.**

ALEXANDER J. CARTWRIGHT 1820-1892

★ **Amateur ball player who wrote baseball's rules; in 1845.**

★ Designed the baseball diamond in 1845; he also umpired the first game played under his rules, on June 19, 1846, in New Jersey.

MARY SHADD CARY 1823-1893

★ **First black newspaperwoman in North America.**

★ In 1853 she was the key figure in starting a weekly newspaper for blacks in the Windsor area. The paper was published until 1859.

DANIEL MAURICE CASEY 1865-1943

★ **He claimed he was the Casey in "Casey at the Bat."**

★ The poem was written by Ernest Laurence Thayer in 1888.

PIERRE CAUCHON D.1442

★ **President of the court that convicted Joan of Arc in 1431.**

ROBERT CAWDREY

★ **He compiled the first English dictionary; in 1604.**

★ It was called *The Table Alphabeticall of Hard Words* and contained brief definitions for its 2,560 entries.

GEORGE (SIR) CAYLEY 1773-1857

★ **Built the first successful glider to carry a human; in 1853.**

★ He was a prolific inventor who invented the caterpillar tractor, artificial limbs, a new type of telescope, and the tension wheel.

MALCOLM GREENE CHACE 1875-1955

★ **Introduced ice hockey to the United States in the 1890s.**

★ Arthur E. Foote, another tennis player, was involved with Chace in the introduction of the game.

HENRY CHADWICK 1824-1908

★ **American sportswriter who compiled the first official rulebook for baseball; in 1869.**

★ It became *Spalding's Official Baseball Guide*.

JAMES CHALMERS

★ **Printed the first stamps in 1834.**

★ He also invented the adhesive postage stamp in 1840; the first was the Penny Black – Queen Victoria on a dark background.

JEAN FRANCOIS CHAMPOLLION 1790-1832

★ **Found key to deciphering hieroglyphics with the aid of the Rosetta Stone; from 1822 to 1824.**

★ French archaelogist who also founded science of Egyptology.

CHARES

★ **Greek sculptor of the Colossus of Rhodes.**

JOHN P. CHARLTON

★ **Invented the postcard in Philadelphia in 1861.**

JOB
CHARNOCK D.1693

★ **Founder of Calcutta, India; in 1690.**
★ He worked as an agent for the East India Co. at the time.

EDNA WOOLMAN
CHASE 1877-1957

★ **She organized first-ever fashion show in the United States, held at the Ritz-Carlton Hotel, New York.**
★ Chase worked for *Vogue* from 1895 to 1957.

CALEB
CHEESHATEAUMUCHK

★ **First North American Indian to receive a degree from Harvard University; in 1665.**

ROBERT
CHESEBROUGH 1837-1933

★ **Manufactured Vaseline Petroleum Jelly; in 1870.**
★ The name Vaseline comes from elain (Greek for oil) and vasser (German for water).

PETER
CHILVERS

★ **Invented the wooden sailboard in 1958.**
★ He did not exploit his invention commercially.

DELPHINE
CHRA

EDDIE
LEVITT

★ **Set a world record for the longest kiss in 1984 — they kissed for 17 days, 10 1/2 hours in Chicago.**

OLE KIRK CHRISTIANSEN

★ **Dane who formed the company Lego in 1932.**
★ The company began to produce the Lego bricks in 1955.

NICOLAS CHUQUET 1445-1500

★ **European mathematician who was the first to understand the concept of negative numbers.**

ELLEN CHURCH

★ **Nurse who became the first stewardess; in 1930.**
★ She worked for United Airlines.

AARON CHWATT 1918-

★ **Real name of comedian Red Buttons.**

DOLORES CLAMAN

★ **She wrote the theme song for "Hockey Night in Canada."**
★ She wrote it in 1968 when she worked at MacLaren Advertising; it's never been published.

GEORGES CLAUDE 1870-1960

★ **French dentist/physicist who invented neon signs; in 1909.**
★ The signs were displayed in public for the first time at the Paris Motor Show in 1910.

FATHER CLÉMENT

★ **Produced clementines by crossing mandarin oranges with Seville oranges; in 1900.**

WILLIAM JOHN CLIFTON 1927-1981

★ **Real name of rock legend Bill Haley.**

SANFORD LOCKWOOD CLUETT 1874-1968

★ **Inventor of Sanforized cloth.**

PHYLLIS COATES

★ **First actress to play Lois Lane on the 50s TV series "The Adventures of Superman."**

★ Coates started in 1951, Noelle Neill followed from 1953 to 1957.

JOSEPHINE GARIS COCHRANE

★ **Invented first automatic dishwasher; in 1886.**

CHRISTOPHER SYDNEY COCKERELL 1910-

★ **English inventor of the hovercraft, patented in 1955.**

CHARLES ALBERT COFFIN 1844-1926

★ **First president of General Electric (1892 to 1922).**

NAOMI
COHEN 1943-1974

★ **Real name of singer Mama Cass Elliot.**

THOMAS WILLIAM
COKE 1754-1842

★ **He commissioned the bowler hat to be made.**
★ It was intended as protective gear for gamekeepers.

MAGDALENA CECILIA
COLLEDGE 1920-

★ **First skater to perform a free-skating program to music.**
★ Also first to do a camel spin and a double jump in competition; the youngest competitor in any Olympics in any sport (1932 Lake Placid Winter Olympics) at 11 years, 76 days.

BARRON GIFT
COLLIER 1873-1939

★ **American ad exec who was the first to put ads in subways.**

VANCE
COLVIG 1892-1967

★ **He did the voices for Pluto and Goofy.**
★ He also did Grumpy and Sleepy in "Snow White."

L.O.
COLVIN

★ **Patented the first vacuum-type milking machine; in 1865.**

CAMMIE KING
CONLON 1935-

★ **She played Bonnie Blue Butler in "Gone With The Wind."**

JAMES B.
CONNOLLY 1869-1957

★ **He was the American athlete who won the first gold medal in the first modern Olympics; in 1896.**

★ He won in triple jump (hop, step, jump) with a distance of 45 feet.

HARRY SAYLES
CONOVER 1911-1965

★ **Model agency owner who created the term "cover girl."**

JACQUES-NICOLAS
CONTE 1755-1805

★ **In 1792, he invented the pencil.**

★ It was made of graphite and clay covered in cedar.

THEODORE JAMES
COOMBS 1954-

★ **He roller-skated 5,193 miles from Los Angeles to New York to Yates Center, Kansas; in 1979.**

★ It took him from May 30 to September 14.

DANIEL M.
COOPER

★ **Invented the employee's punch clock; in 1894.**

KENNETH H.
COOPER

★ **He coined the term "aerobics" in 1968.**

★ U.S. Air Force major with a doctorate in exercise physiology assigned to develop a drill for physical conditioning for recruits.

MERIAN C. COOPER 1895-1973

★ **Conceived, produced, and directed "King Kong" in 1933.**

GEORGE CORMACK 1870-1953

★ **The inventor of Wheaties cereal; in 1924.**
★ He was head miller at the predecessor of General Mills.

WILLIAM EPPS CORMACK 1796-1868

★ **He was the first European to cross Newfoundland on foot as he explored its interior; in 1822.**

CHARLOTTE CORNWELL

★ **Sister of John le Carré who was the model for Charlie in *The Little Drummer Girl.***

CHARLES J. CORRELL 1890-1972

★ **Played Andy in "Amos 'n' Andy" on radio.**

ANETA CORSAUT

★ **Actress who played Helen Crump on "The Andy Griffith Show" from 1964 to 1968.**

OTTO FRIEDRICH W. COSSEL

★ **First piano teacher to Johannes Brahms.**

KAMI COTLER

★ **Actress who played youngest daughter, Elizabeth, on "The Waltons" from 1972 to 1981.**

EMILE COUÉ 1857-1926

★ **French psychotherapist who introduced the phrase "Day by day, in every way, I am getting better and better"; in 1923.**

ERNEST KENT COULTER 1871-1952

★ **Founder of the Big Brothers of America; in 1946.**

JOSHUA LIONEL COWEN 1880-1965

★ **Created Lionel trains.**

EDWIN W. COX

★ **Responsible for developing SOS pads; in 1917.**

★ SOS stands for Save Our Saucepans.

CHARLES CREIGHTON 1908-1970

★ **He and James Hargis drove from New York to Los Angeles in reverse without stopping the engine once; in 1930.**

★ They returned to New York in reverse. They left July 22, arrived in Los Angeles on August 13, and were back in New York by September 5, for a round-trip total of 7,180 miles in 42 days.

BARTOLOMMEO DI FRANCESCO
CRISTOFORI 1655-1731

★ **He built the first piano; in 1720 in Italy.**

SUZANNE
CROUGH

★ **She played Tracy Partridge on "The Partridge Family."**

GEORGE
CRUM

★ **Chef who first made potato chips; in 1853.**

NICHOLAS JOSEPH
CUGNOT

★ **He built the first automobile; in 1771.**
★ Credited by the British and French automobile clubs as the builder of the first true automobile, a steam-powered tricycle that carried four people and ran for 20 minutes at 2 1/4 m.p.h.

MICHAEL "MIKE"
CULLEN

★ **Opened the first supermarket in 1930**
★ It was the King Kullen, in Jamaica, New York.

PIERRE "PEYO"
CULLIFORD D.1992

★ **Belgian cartoonist who created the Smurfs in 1957.**

WILLIAM ARTHUR "CANDY"
CUMMINGS 1848-1924

★ **The originator of baseball's curve ball; in the 1860s.**

JOHN CUNNINGHAM

★ **He took the first jet airliner (the deHavilland Comet) on its maiden flight; in 1917.**

AUSTEN M. CURTIS 1890-1945

★ **First to hear words spoken over the transatlantic telephone.**

★ The call took place in 1915 from Arlington, Virginia, to Paris.

SONNY CURTIS

★ **He sang the catchy theme "Love Is All Around" for "The Mary Tyler Moore Show."**

★ Pat Williams composed the song.

★ Curtis was also an original member of Buddy Holly's Crickets.

PETER CUZIMANO

★ **He started the tradition of throwing an octopus on the ice in hockey games played in Detroit.**

★ Seafood shop owner who in 1951-52 season threw an octopus to encourage the Red Wings to extend their seven-game winning streak to eight games—the octopus has eight legs.

LEON F. CZOLGOSZ 1873-1901

★ **Anarchist who assassinated President McKinley in 1901 at the Pan-American Exposition in Buffalo, New York.**

★ McKinley was the 25th president and was only six months into his second term as president. Czolgosz was electrocuted in 1901.

IVA TOGURI D'AQUINO 1916-

★ **One of the "Tokyo Rose" broadcasters.**
★ An American typist, she was the only one imprisoned for treason. She was sentenced to 10 years, was fined $10,000, deprived of her U.S. citizenship, released in 1956, and pardoned in 1977.

GUIDO D'AREZZO 995-1050

★ **Italian musician and singing teacher who formed the basis for musical notation — do,re,mi,fa... ; in the 11th century.**

ROLAND E. DAAB 1914-

★ **Attended Sunday School for 3,675 consecutive Sundays.**
★ That is more than 70 years.

ALLAN ROY DAFOE 1883-1943

★ **Delivered the Dionne quintuplets in 1934 in Ontario.**

GARY DAHL

★ **The creator of pet rocks, a fad of the mid-70s.**
★ He invented them in response to friends who complained about the expense and inconvenience of traditional pets.

JOHN EMERICH EDWARD DALBERG-ACTON 1834-1902

★ **English historian who wrote "Power tends to corrupt and absolute power corrupts absolutely."**

NILS GUSTAF
DALEN 1869-1937

★ **Swedish physicist and inventor who developed the automatic sun valve used on buoys and unmanned lighthouses.**
★ He also invented the Aga stove.

THOMAS RUDOLF
DALLMEYER

★ **In 1891, he patented the first telephoto lens.**

CARL PETER HENRIK
DAM 1895-1976

★ **Discovered Vitamin K; in 1934 (with Edward A. Doisy).**
★ Vitamin K is important in the regulation of liver function.

CHARLES ANDERSON
DANA 1819-1897

★ **Newspaperman who wrote "When a dog bites a man that is not news, but when a man bites a dog that is news".**
★ It appeared in the New York *Sun* in 1882.

WILLIAM HENRY
DANFORTH 1870-1955

★ **Founder of Ralston Purina Co.**

HART PEASE
DANKS 1834-1903

★ **Wrote "Silver Threads Among the Gold"; in 1873.**
★ U.S. singer and composer who wrote the song as a tribute to his wife, but seemingly to no avail — they separated the next year.

FREDERICK DANNAY / **MANFRED B. LEE**

★ **Cousins who wrote under the pseudonym of Ellery Queen.**

VIRGINIA DARE 1587-1587

★ **First English child born in America; on August 18, 1587.**
★ She was born on Roanoke Island, the first English settlement.

CHARLES B. DARROW 1889-1967

★ **Creator of Monopoly; in 1933.**
★ Parker Brothers rejected it, saying it was dull, slow-paced, and complex. A department store agreed to stock it. It sold so well that Parker Brothers bought the rights, but after a year of sales, a cautious executive ordered that no more games be made. The copyright reverted to Darrow and he went on to make a fortune.

RAYMOND ARTHUR DART 1893-1988

★ **Australian anthropologist who discovered the "missing link" in the evolutionary chain; in 1924.**

DENISE ANN DARVALL 1942-1967

★ **Donor of the heart used for the first heart transplant.**
★ The operation was performed by Christiaan Barnard on Louis Washansky in 1967; the patient died 18 days later.

ADI DASSLER 1900-1978

★ **Shoemaker who started Adidas ; in the 1920s.**

WILLIAM DAVENANT 1606-1668

★ **Considered to be the illegitimate child of William Shakespeare.**

★ Records indicate he was the son of an innkeeper. Shakespeare stopped there frequently, giving rise to the rumour that he was the child's father. At age 12, Davenant wrote "Ode in the Remembrance of Master Shakespeare," adding fuel to the fire.

JACK LLEWELYN DAVIES 1894-1959

★ **J.M. Barrie's model for John Darling in *Peter Pan*.**

VALENTINE DAVIES 1905-

★ **Screenwriter who wrote "Miracle on 34th Street" and won the Academy Award for original story.**

WILLIAM DAWES 1745-1799

★ **Rode along with Paul Revere in warning the colonists of the British attack; in 1775.**

★ A third rider was Samuel Prescott (1751-1777).

STEPHEN DAY c.1594-1668

★ **First printer in the English colonies in America.**

★ The book printed was the Psalms.

GARCIA LOPEZ DE CARDENAS

★ **He discovered the Grand Canyon in 1540.**

CHARLES
DE L'ECLUSE 1526-1609

★ **He sent the first European tulips to Holland, beginning the development of the famous Dutch tulips.**

JUAN
DE LA CIERVA 1896-1936

★ **Invented the autogyro in 1919, forerunner of the helicopter.**
★ Spanish engineer who was killed in a commercial aircraft crash.

CARL GUSTAV PATRIK
DE LAVAL

★ **Swedish inventor of the turbine-operated centrifugal cream separator in 1878.**

ADRAGON EASTWOOD
DE MELLO 1976-

★ **He got his BA in Mathematics from the University of California at age 11 years 8 months in 1988.**

GEORGE
DE MESTRAL

★ **Swiss mountaineer who invented Velcro; in 1948.**
★ The name comes from velvet and crochet.

JEAN PILATRE
DE ROSIER

★ **Undertook the first manned balloon flight in 1783.**
★ The flight was made in the Montgolfier brothers' hot air balloon. He flew five and a half miles in 20 minutes.

DELPHINE DELAMARE

★ **French woman on whom Flaubert based the title charcter in *Madame Bovary*.**

JEAN JOSEPH DELAMBRE 1749-1822

★ **Made the measure that legally defined the metre; in 1791.**

★ Pierre Mechain (1744-1804) worked with him.

JEAN-BAPTISTE DENIS

★ **He performed the first blood transfusion; in 1667.**

★ The blood was lamb's blood and was given to a 15-year-old boy, who recovered from his ailment.

JOHANN CHRISTOPH DENNER 1655-1707

★ **Invented the clarinet; in Germany in 1670.**

ALBERT DESALVO D.1973

★ **The real name of the Boston Strangler.**

HENRY JOHN DEUTSCHENDORF, JR. 1943-

★ **Real name of singer John Denver.**

AMELIA DEVINE

★ **First woman Salvation Army bell-ringer in the United States.**

LOUIS FELIX
DIAT 1885-1957

★ **Chef of the Ritz-Carlton Hotel in New York who created vichysoisse.**

EARLE ENSIGN
DICKSON 1893-1961

★ **Invented Band-Aids.**
★ His wife was accident prone so he had made dressings that would stay in place, were easy to apply, and were sterile.

WILLIAM KENNEDY LAURIE
DICKSON 1860-1935

★ **The first film director.**
★ Directed Edison's first films in 1889.

HOWARD
DIETZ

★ **Advertising man responsible for making the lion the trademark for Goldwyn Pictures (became MGM); in 1896.**

SHIRLEY
DINSDALE

★ **Puppeteer who won the first Emmy in 1948 as "Most Outstanding Television Personality."**
★ Her puppet was called Judy Splinters.

KONRAD
DIPPEL 1673-1734

★ **Mary Shelly based Victor Frankenstein on him.**
★ Dippel, who spent his youth at Castle Frankenstein, believed the spirit could leave the body and return.

RUDOLPH
DIRKS 1877-1968

★ **Created the Katzenjammer Kids; in 1897.**

★ They are the longest-lived characters in American comic strips.

THOMAS
DIXON 1864-1946

★ **Author of the book on which *Birth of a Nation* was based.**

★ The book, *The Clansman* (1905), defended the Ku Klux Klan.

CONRAD S.
DOBER 1891-1938

★ **Wrote the music for "The Continental," which won the first Oscar for a song in 1934.**

★ The lyrics for "The Continental" were by Herb Magidson.

LAWRENCE EUGENE
DOBY 1924-

★ **He was the second black player in the major leagues, following Jackie Robinson.**

★ He was the first black player in the American League; with Cleveland Indians in 1947.

JAMES
DODD 1910-1964

★ **Host of the Mickey Mouse Club.**

★ He also wrote the theme song, "Mickey Mouse March."

SONORA SMART
DODD

★ **She established the tradition of Father's Day; in 1910.**

JAMES DRUMMOND
DOLE 1877-1958

★ **Founder of the Hawaiian pineapple industry.**

WILLIAM RICHARD
DOLL 1912-

★ **English physician who proved the link between lung cancer and cigarette smoking.**

LYNN
DOLLAR

★ **Escorted people into the isolation booth on "The $64,000 Question"; from 1955 to 1958.**

THOMAS ALOYSIUS
DORGAN 1877-1929

★ **Cartoonist who introduced term "hot dog"; in 1906.**
★ Sausages sold in buns were called "red hot daschund sausages." He wanted to draw a cartoon of the sausages but he couldn't spell daschund so he chose "dog." Instead of daschunds, he drew miniature poodles inside buns.

RHETA CHILDE
DORR 1866-1948

★ **First female war correspondent; in World War I.**

JAMES
DOUGHERTY

★ **First husband of Marilyn Monroe.**
★ They were married from 1942 to 1946.

ANDREW ELLICOTT DOUGLASS 1867-1962

★ **Developed science of reading tree rings for dating.**

★ American astronomer; called the method "dendrochronology."

THOMAS (CAPTAIN) DOVER 1660-1742

★ **Rescued the real Robinson Crusoe (Alexander Selkirk) on whom Defoe based his famous novel.**

★ English physician; invented Dover's Powder to provoke sweating.

EDWIN LAURENTINE DRAKE 1819-1880

★ **Drilled the first oil well in the United States; in Titusville, Pennsylvania in 1859.**

★ Railway conductor who struck oil after three months of drilling; he lost all his money in oil speculation by 1863.

CORNELIUS JACOBZOON DREBBEL 1572-1633

★ **Dutchman who built first navigable submarine; in 1620.**

★ It was powered by 12 rowers who remained underwater for several hours, breathing an artificial gas (oxygen) he made.

RICHARD CHARLES DREW 1904-1950

★ **Operated first blood bank in 1940 in New York City.**

★ Black American surgeon who established that blood plasma could replace whole blood in transfusions. He directed the American Red Cross blood program in 1941 and resigned the same year when the Red Cross complied with an Armed Forces' directive to segregate the blood.

DICK DREW

★ **In 1925, he invented adhesive tape.**

★ It was marketed as Scotch tape. Initially intended to help paint cars in two tones as it didn't lift off the paint when removed.

PHILIP DRINKER 1894-1972

★ **Invented the iron lung; in 1928.**

★ First model contained parts of two household vacuum cleaners.

ARCHIE DUNCAN 1914-1979

★ **Played "Little John" in the 50s TV series "Robin Hood."**

DONALD F. DUNCAN 1893-1971

★ **Marketed the yo-yo as a toy in 1926.**

★ It was a Phillipine weapon/hunting aid.

LEE DUNCAN 1893-1960

★ **Original owner and trainer of Rin-Tin-Tin.**

★ He owned and trained all four generations of Rin-Tin-Tins.

GEORGE DUNNING 1920-

★ **Canadian animator responsible for the movie "Yellow Submarine" (1968).**

JOHN C. DUNTON

★ **Invented the first jukebox that gave a choice of music to be selected by the user; in 1905.**

★ There were 24 records to choose from. An earlier jukebox did not allow you to choose what you wanted to hear — you deposited your nickel in the slot and got what was in the machine.

AMANDINE LUCIE AURORE DUPIN 1804-1876

★ **Real name of George Sand.**

FANNY DURACK 1892-1956

★ **Australian swimmer who was the first woman to win an Olympic gold medal in any sport; in 1912.**

★ She won the 100 m freestyle, in which she set a world record.

PIERRE DURAND

★ **Patented a metalled vessel for preserving food in 1810. He called his invention a tin cannister.**

WILLIAM CRAPO DURANT 1862-1947

★ **Founder of General Motors Corp.**

★ He organized the Buick Motor Company in 1905 and consolidated it with smaller companies to create GM in 1910.

IOSIF VISSARIONOVICH DZHUGASHVILI 1879-1953

★ **Real name of Joseph Stalin.**

EDWARD P.F. EAGAN 1898-1967

★ **One of the few athletes who have gold medals in two different sports.**

★ American athlete; he won for boxing in the 1920 Summer Olympics and for bobsledding in the 1932 Winter Olympics.

B. REEVES EASON 1886-1956

★ **He directed the chariot race and the sea battle in the 1926 version of "Ben Hur."**

★ The film set a record in 1926 for its cost — $4 million.

KEVIN EASTMAN PETER LAIRD

★ **Creators of Teenage Mutant Ninja Turtles; in 1983.**

★ At the time Laird was an illustrator of vegetables for a newspaper garden section and Eastman was a short-order cook.

HUBERT LEWBRIGHT EATON 1881-1966

★ **The founder and designer of Forest Lawn Cemetery in Glendale, California; in 1916.**

★ It was the world's first memorial park. When it opened, it covered 50 acres; today its 1,200 acres are spread over four parks.

NATHANIEL EATON 1609-1674

★ **Appointed first head of Harvard University in 1636.**

★ He was removed from office for cruelty and financial irregularities.

GERTRUDE CAROLINE
EDERLE 1906-

★ **First woman to swim the English Channel; in 1926.**
★ American who broke the existing men's record by 2 hours. Also won a gold medal and two bronzes in the 1924 Olympics.

SARAH EMMA EVELYN
EDMONDS 1841-1898

★ **She fought in the Civil War disguised as a man.**
★ As Frank Thompson, she was a Union soldier at the first Battle of Bull Run (1861) and in Fredericksburg (1862).

CLIFF
EDWARDS 1895-1971

★ **Actor who was the voice of Jiminy Cricket and Pinocchio.**

JOHN
ELKHAY

★ **Made a record 315 two-egg omelettes in 30 minutes; in 1985.**

WILLIAM WEBB
ELLIS 1805-1872

★ **Inventor of rugby; in 1823.**
★ As a pupil at Rugby School in 1823, he broke the rules by picking up the ball and running with it during a game of association football, thus inspiring the new game of rugby.

LINCOLN
ELLSWORTH 1880-1951

★ **First man to fly across both polar regions.**
★ He flew over the North Pole in 1926 and the South Pole in 1935.

EUGENE ELY

★ **He made the first aircraft take-off from the deck of a warship in 1910.**

★ He made the first landing on a ship two months later (it was on a different mission).

DAVID AND ELIZABETH EMANUEL

★ **Designed Lady Diana's wedding gown.**

DANIEL DECATUR EMMETT 1815-1904

★ **Northern minstrel and songwriter who wrote "Dixie" in 1859.**

JOHN FRANKLIN ENDERS 1897-1985

★ **Isolated the measles virus; in 1962.**

★ American microbiologist who also perfected a vaccine against polio with two other researchers; discovered method to culture viruses outside living bodies.

DOUGLAS ENGELBART

★ **Conceived and designed the computer "mouse" in 1965.**

JULIUS J. AND PHILIP G. EPSTEIN

★ **Twin brothers responsible for the screenwriting of "Casablanca."**

★ Julius: 1909-; Philip 1909-1952.

EDVARD
ERICKSEN 1877-1959

★ **Sculptor of "The Little Mermaid" in Copenhagen.**

ERNEST
ESCLANGON 1876-1954

★ **Invented a "speaking clock"– a telephone number you could call to be told the time; in 1934.**
★ It was the first time people could call a phone number and hear a recorded message.

PHILIP
ESTRIDGE

★ **Headed the team that developed the IBM PC in 1981.**

JOHN
ETHERINGTON

★ **English haberdasher who wore the first top hat; in 1797.**
★ The first time he wore the hat, a large crowd assembled causing a shoving match. He was arrested for disturbing the peace but within a month he was swamped with orders.

HERBERT McLEAN
EVANS 1883-1971

★ **Discovered Vitamin E in 1922.**
★ K.S. Bishop aided in the discovery.

PERCIVAL "PERCY"
EVERITT

★ **Patented a coin-operated weighing machine; in 1884.**

FRANCOIS FABER 1887-1915

★ **First non-Frenchman to win the Tour de France bicycle race; in 1909.**

★ He was from Luxembourg.

ELEANORA FAGAN 1915-1959

★ **Real name of Billie Holliday, blues singer.**

CONSTANTINE FAHLBERG

★ **Discoverer of saccharin; in 1879.**

★ Professor Ira Remsen aided in the discovery. It was patented in 1885 and is the sweetest substance on earth.

EMILY FAITHFULL 1835-1895

★ **Started all-female printing firms to employ woman.**

★ First was started in 1857 in Edinburgh, second in 1860 in London.

STARR FAITHFULL D.1929

★ **Nymphomaniac whose life was fictionalized in John O'Hara's *Butterfield 8.***

BENOIT FALCHETTO

★ **He drove the car in which dancer Isadora Duncan died when her scarf got caught in the wheels.**

HUGH

FALCONER 1808-1865

★ **Scottish botanist who introduced tea plants to India.**

ALBERT BACON

FALL 1861-1944

★ **U.S. Cabinet member who accepted the bribe that led to the Teapot Dome Scandal.**

★ He was the first cabinet officer convicted of a felony while in office. He was the Secretary of the Interior from 1921 to 1923 and was convicted in 1929 of accepting a $100,000 bribe.

AGNETHA

FALTSKOG

★ **One of the "A"s in pop group ABBA.**

★ The other A is Anni-Frid Lyngstad, and the "B"s are Bjorn Ulvaeus and Benny Andersson.

JEAN-BAPTISTE

FARINA 1685-1766

★ **He was an Italian barber who created eau-de-Cologne in Cologne; in 1709.**

HENRI

FARMAN 1874-1958

★ **Took the first air passenger up, flying over Paris; in 1908.**

★ The passenger was his brother Maurice.

SELM ALEXANDER

FAULKNER 1936-

★ **The first Newfoundlander to play in the N.H.L.**

★ Played with Detroit Red Wings in 1962.

FREDERICK SCHILLER

FAUST 1892-1944

★ **Wrote the "Dr. Kildare" short stories.**

LEONARDO

FIBONACCI c.1170-c.1230

★ **Primarily responsible for the European adoption of Arabic numerals (from India).**

★ Italian mathematician; also responsible for discovering Fibonacci numbers — numbers that form a sequence in which each number is the sum of its two predecessors: 1, 1, 2, 3, 5, 8, 13....

JAMES

FIGG c.1695-1734

★ **Winner of the first title fight, which took place in London, England; in 1727.**

★ English fencer and pugilist who defeated Ned Sutton in this fight.

COLIN GARFIELD

FINK 1882-1953

★ **He discovered the tungsten filament, which made the mass production of light bulbs possible.**

TULA ELLICE

FINKLEA 1921-

★ **Real name of actress/dancer Cyd Charisse.**

JAMES MONTGOMERY

FLAGG 1877-1960

★ **Drew World War I Uncle Sam recruiting poster.**

★ The illustration first appeared as a magazine cover.

ROBERT JOSEPH
FLAHERTY 1884-1951

★ **Explorer and movie producer who made the first documentary film, "Nanook of the North"; in 1922.**

JOHN
FLAMSTEED 1646-1719

★ **In 1675 he became the first Astronomer Royal.**

FRANK AND HENRY
FLEER

★ **Developed bubble gum (Double Bubble); in 1928.**

★ Frank's first effort was called Blibber-Blubber Bubble Gum but was a failure because it burst before the bubble was big enough and it was too wet. Henry developed Chiclets in 1910.

ARTHUR
FLEGENHEIMER 1902-1935

★ **Real name of gangster "Dutch" Schultz.**

HORACE
FLETCHER 1849-1919

★ **Started idea of chewing your food at least 32 times.**

★ This method of eating was called "Fletcherizing." The practice was believed to be necessary because Americans gobbled their food and generally had poor dietary habits.

JOHN
FLETCHER 1579-1625

★ **He collaborated with Shakespeare on "Henry VIII."**

★ English dramatist.

WILLIAM MITCHELL FOLBERTH

★ **Invented windshield wipers that worked automatically, using compressed air; in 1921.**

ROBERT FORD D.1892

★ **Killer of Jesse James in 1882.**
★ Earned $10,000 reward; was gunned down 10 years later.

NATHAN BEDFORD FORREST 1821-1877

★ **Confederate general who was the first Grand Wizard of the original Ku Klux Klan.**
★ It was founded in 1865 and disbanded in 1869.

ROBERT FOULIS 1796-1866

★ **Designed a steam-powered foghorn; in 1853.**
★ Bells had been in use up to that time but the foghorn could be heard for miles, sending out coded sounds so a navigator could tell what piece of land the ship was near. It was patented by an American who benefited financially; Foulis died in poverty.

GEORGE FOX 1624-1691

★ **Founder of the Society of Friends (Quakers).**

HERBERT ERNST KARL FRAHM 1913-

★ **Real name of ex-German chancellor Willy Brandt.**

BERTHA LEE FRANKLIN

★ **Woman who killed singer Sam Cooke; in Los Angeles, December 11, 1964.**

JAMES EARLE FRASER 1876-1953

★ **American sculptor who designed the Buffalo nickel that was minted from 1913 to 1938.**

PAUL FREES

★ **Was the voice of John Beresford Tipton on "The Millionaire."**
★ Also Boris Badenov on the "Rocky and Bullwinkle Show."

DANIEL CHESTER FRENCH 1850-1931

★ **Sculptor of the statue of Lincoln in the Lincoln Memorial.**

CHARLES FREY

★ **Invented the first fruit machine; in 1889.**
★ It was called the Liberty Bell and its payout ranged from one coin for two horseshoes to two coins for three bells.

FRANÇOIS FRÉZIER

★ **Discovered a Chilean strawberry that led to the cultivation of modern strawberries.**
★ In 1714 he brought the Chilean strawberry to Brittany where it was crossed with the Virginia strawberry.

FLORIDA
FRIEBUS

★ **Actress who played Dobie Gillis's mother Winifred in TV's "The Many Loves of Dobie Gillis."**

★ His father Herbert T. Gillis was played by Frank Faylen.

ESTHER PAULINE AND PAULINE ESTHER
FRIEDMAN 1918-

★ **Former is Ann Landers, latter is her twin sister, Abigail Van Buren, who writes the Dear Abby column.**

★ Ann's nickname is Eppie; Abby's is Popo.

SAMILE DIANE
FRIESEN 1937-

★ **Real name of actress Dyan Cannon.**

HELGE
FRIHOLM 1910-

★ **As of June 1989, she had collected 54,540 different beer caps from around the world.**

FRIEDRICH AUGUST WILHELM
FROEBEL 1782-1852

★ **He was the German founder of the kindergarten system, starting in 1837.**

JAMES ANTHONY
FROUDE 1818-1894

★ **English historian and traveller who was the first to use the term "down under" to describe Australia; in 1886.**

ART
FRY

★ **Creator of Post-it Notes.**
★ After 3M dismissed an adhesive that had very little sticking power, chemist Fry used the glue to make removable book marks. It took Fry until 1980 to convince 3M that they were overlooking a great idea.

SARAH JANE
FULKS 1914-

★ **Real name of actress Jane Wyman.**

CASIMIR
FUNK 1884-1967

★ **Invented the word "vitamin"; in 1912.**
★ The name comes from "vital amines"; an amine is an ammonia-based organic compound.

ASHRITA
FURMAN

★ **Walked 32.9 miles balancing a full pint milk bottle on her forehead; in 1989.**

ELDA
FURRY 1890-1966

★ **Real name of Hollywood columnist Hedda Hopper.**

JOHANN
FUST c.1400-1466

★ **Partner and financier of Johann Gutenberg.**
★ At the end of their partnership, he sued Gutenberg for payment and got possession of printing press in lieu of payment.

DENNIS GABOR 1900-1979

★ **Discoverer of the holograph.**

★ Hungarian-born British physicist who also invented a colour TV tube in 1958 that was more compact than any up to that time.

WILLIAM M. GAINES

★ **Founder and publisher of *Mad* magazine.**

FRANZ JOSEPH GALL 1758-1828

★ **German physician who founded the pseudoscience of phrenology.**

★ Phrenology is a study of the variations in skull shape that are believed to determine a person's character.

JOHANN GOTTFRIED GALLE 1812-1910

★ **The German astronomer who discovered the planet Neptune; in 1846.**

★ Urbain Leverrier had predicted its existence and position.

FRANCIS GALTON 1822-1911

★ **English founder of eugenics; coined the term in 1883.**

★ Eugenics is the belief that physical and mental attributes in humans could be controlled and improved by selective breeding.

★ He also founded the modern technique of weather mapping (1863) and was an early advocate of using fingerprints for identification.

JOHN
GAMGEE

★ **Installed the first artificial skating rink; in London in 1876.**
★ He called it a Glacarium; it was in King's Road, Chelsea.

ABEL / ANDRÉ
GANCE / DEBRIE

★ **The French film makers who invented stereophonic sound for motion pictures.**

JACQUELINE
GAREAU

★ **Proclaimed the winner of the Boston Marathon when it was found that the supposed winner Rosie Ruiz had cheated.**

MAURICE
GARIN

★ **The first winner of the Tour de France bicycle race; in 1903.**

ANDRÉ JACQUES
GARNERIN 1769-1823

★ **Frenchman who patented the parachute in 1802.**
★ He made his first jump from a balloon at a height of 2,230 feet in Paris in 1797. The balloon was based on a design by Da Vinci but it had no hole in the top so it swayed violently from side to side.

ELBERT HENRY
GARY 1846-1927

★ **American lawyer after whom Gary, Indiana, is named.**
★ He was one of the founders of U.S. Steel in 1901.

MATEJ
GASPAR 1987-

★ **Named the world's 5 billionth inhabitant by the U.N.**
★ He was born in Zagreb, Yugoslavia.

PIERRE
GASSENDI 1592-1655

★ **He introduced the term "aurora borealis" in 1621.**

DAVE
GAUDER

★ **Single-handedly pulled the Concorde 40 feet across the tarmac of Heathrow Airport; in 1987.**

ALEXANDER
GAUGE

★ **This actor played Friar Tuck in '50s TV series "The Adventures of Robin Hood."**

JOSEPH C.
GAYETTY

★ **Invented toilet paper; in 1857.**
★ He was the first to sell commercially packaged toilet paper; it was sold in individual sheets. Up to this time, people used old catalogues, newspapers, and other paper products.

GEE JON D.1924

★ **The first man to be executed in a gas chamber; at Nevada State Prison.**
★ He was a member of a tong, a Chinese gang.

ED
GEIN

★ **Norman Bates in *Psycho* was based on this Wisconsin farmhand whose activities were toned down for the film.**

THEODOR
GEISEL 1904-1991

★ **Wrote children's books under the name Dr. Seuss.**

MURRAY
GELL-MANN 1929-

★ **American physicist who formulated the theory of the quark; in 1963.**
★ The quark is the smallest particle in the universe.

JAC SIDNEY (DR.)
GELLER

★ **Performed first successful separation of Siamese twins.**
★ The operation took place on December 14, 1952, in Cleveland. The girls were joined at the sternum and survived for one year.

HEIDI AND LAURA
GENTRY

★ **The first pair of twins who played baby Tabitha on "Bewitched"; in 1966.**

STEVE
GERBER

★ **Created Howard the Duck; in 1972.**
★ The film "Howard the Duck" replaced Heaven's Gate as the biggest movie flop to that time. It cost $40 million to make.

WILLIAM FREDERICK GERICKE

★ **First used the term hydroponics; in 1929 in California.**

ELBRIDGE GERRY 1744-1814

★ **American after whom "gerrymandering" is named.**
★ It is the rearranging of electoral districts for political advantage.
★ He was vice-president for President Madison from 1812 to 1814 after being governor of Massachusetts from 1810 to 1811.

ABRAHAM GESNER 1797-1864

★ **Canadian who invented kerosene (coal oil) in 1846.**
★ He coined the word kerosene from two Greek words meaning wax and oil. The new fuel was first used to light a lighthouse.

JAMES GIBB

★ **Invented table tennis; in 1926.**
★ He also introduced the celluloid ball that's used in the game.

CEDRIC GIBBONS 1895-1960

★ **Designed the Oscar statuette; in 1927.**
★ He was also the head of the MGM art department from 1924 to 1956; created sets for 2,000 films; and won 11 Academy Awards.

WILLIAM GIBBONS

★ **Took out the first life insurance policy in the world; in 1583 in England.**

HENRI
GIFFARD 1825-1882

★ **Invented the passenger-carrying dirigible; in 1852.**
★ It had 3 h.p. steam engine and 11-foot propeller, went 17 miles.

GARY
GIGAX

★ **Created the controversial Dungeons and Dragons in 1973.**
★ He and his co-creator were inspired by *Lord of the Rings.*

ALFRED CARLTON
GILBERT 1884-1961

★ **Created the Erector Set.**

HUMPHREY
GILBERT 1537-1583

★ **He founded the first North American English colony in 1583.**
★ It was at the present-day St. John's, Newfoundland.

HAVEN
GILLESPIE

J. FRED
COOTS

★ **Wrote "Santa Claus Is Comin' to Town"; in 1934.**

EDNA RAE
GILOOLEY 1932-

★ **Real name of actress Ellen Burstyn.**

CHRISTOPHER
GIST c.1706-1759

★ **Rescued George Washington from drowning in 1753.**
★ U.S. explorer and scout; also first white American to explore the Ohio Valley; in 1750.

CHARLES JASPER
GLIDDEN 1856-1927

★ **He organized the first telephone exchange; in Lowell, Massachusetts, in 1877.**

JOSEPH FARWELL
GLIDDEN 1813-1906

★ **Devised a machine to make barbed wire; patented in 1873.**

AVRON HIRSCH
GOLBOGEN 1909-1958

★ **Real name of U.S. film producer Mike Todd.**
★ He was Elizabeth Taylor's third husband; he died in a plane crash.

SYLVAN
GOLDMAN

★ **In 1937 he invented the first supermarket cart.**
★ It was a folding carrier with wheels that held two baskets.

PETER CARL
GOLDMARK 1906-1977

★ **Developed 33 1/3 long-playing phonograph records; in 1948.**
★ Also the first successful colour television system in 1940.

LYLE DAVID
GOODHUE

★ **He patented the aerosol; in 1941.**

JULIE
GOODYEAR 1945-

★ **English actress best known for her part as the glamorous Bet Lynch Gilroy in "Coronation Street."**

MARGARET GORMAN 1905-

★ **Winner of the first Miss America Pageant; in 1921.**

★ Her vital statistics were 30-25-32; height: 5'1"; weight: 108 pounds; age: 16 years old.

JOHN GORRIE

★ **Patented the process for mechanical refrigeration; in 1851.**

RICHARD GRAFTON c.1513-1572

★ **English printer who wrote "Thirty days has November, April, June and September..."; in 1570.**

★ He also issued the first edition of the Book of Common Prayer (1549); wrote three histories of England; and sat in Parliament.

FLORENCE NIGHTINGALE GRAHAM 1878-1966

★ **Real name of Elizabeth Arden, cosmetics manufacturer.**

SYLVESTER GRAHAM 1794-1851

★ **Graham bread and Graham crackers were named after him.**

★ He tried to change the "sinful" eating habits of Americans by promoting whole wheat flour; he claimed that graham crackers contained all essential nutrients and were a cure for alcoholism.

GEORGE F. GRANT

★ **The inventor of the golf tee; in 1899 in Boston.**

WILLIAM WEST GRANT

★ **Performed the first successful appendix operation; in 1885.**

★ His patient was a 22-year-old Iowa farm girl, Mary Gartside.

JEAN FRANÇOIS GRAVELET 1824-1897

★ **First man to cross Niagara Falls on a tightrope; in 1859.**

★ The rope was 3 inches thick, 1100 feet long, and 160 feet above the falls.

ELISHA GRAY 1835-1901

★ **Surprisingly, the inventor of the telephone.**

★ Gray patented his phone only hours after Bell did his. Western Union Telegraph acquired Gray's patent and a lengthy legal battle ensued, which Bell won.

GILDA GRAY 1901-1959

★ **Credited with inventing the dance the "shimmy" in the 1920s.**

GEORGE F. GREEN

★ **Patented the first battery-powered dentist drill; in 1875 in Kalamazoo, Michigan.**

★ Electric-powered dental drills were not introduced until 1908.

ROBERT M. GREEN

★ **Created the ice cream soda; in 1874.**

CHESTER
GREENWOOD

★ **In 1873, he invented ear muffs.**

★ He was 15 when he asked his grandmother to sew chunks of beaver fur onto the ends of a wire.

JOHN
GREENWOOD 1760-1819

★ **American dentist who made George Washington's dentures.**

★ They were made of ivory not wood.

MARC
GRÉGOIRE

★ **Founded the T-fal company in 1956.**

★ Invented the method for encrusting metal with Teflon; applied it to kitchen utensils, starting with the frying pan. The rest is history.

HANSON CROCKETT
GREGORY

★ **Responsible for putting the hole in the doughnut.**

★ He was an American sea captain.

NEHEMIAH
GREW 1641-1712

★ **Discovered Epsom salts; in 1695.**

BURLEIGH ARLAND
GRIMES 1893-1985

★ **Last legal spitball pitcher in the major leagues.**

★ He was one of the few pitchers allowed to throw the spitball after it was banned in 1920.

JOHN AND MYRTLE
GRUELLE

★ **They created the Raggedy Ann doll in 1914.**
★ They made the doll for their daughter Marcella who had tuberculosis. After her death two years later, her father wrote the stories about the doll in his daughter's memory; they were published in 1918, the year the doll went into mass production.

LIONEL
GUEST

H.O.
MERRIMAN

★ **Invented the microphone used to record the first electrical recording ever made; in 1920.**

OCTAVIA
GUILLEN

ADRIANA
MARTINEZ

★ **Were engaged for 67 years before they got married.**
★ Married in Mexico City, in June 1969; both were 82.

MARY LOUISE CECILIA "TEXAS"
GUINAN 1884-1933

★ **Responsible for observation "Fifty million Frenchman can't be wrong"; in New York *World-Telegram*; on March 21, 1931.**

BENO
GUTENBERG

★ **Collaborated with Charles Richter in developing the Richter scale to measure the intensity of earthquakes.**

JAY
GWALTNEY

★ **He ate a birch tree in 1980.**
★ It was 11 feet long and 4.7 inches around. It took him 89 hours.

WALTER C. HAKANSON

★ **Coined the name "Softball"; in 1926.**

★ The game was invented by George W. Hancock in 1887 but was called, among other names, Kitten Ball and Playground Ball.

★ First played as a special Thansksgiving Day event in Chicago.

SARAH JOSEPHA HALE 1788-1879

★ **Responsible for getting the last Thursday in November (Thanksgiving) declared a U.S. national holiday; in 1863.**

★ Magazine editor who also wrote "Mary Had a Little Lamb" (1830).

STEPHEN HALES 1677-1761

★ **He was the first to measure blood pressure.**

★ English botanist who also invented a machine for preserving meat and a machine for distilling sea water.

BENJAMIN HALL

★ **The person after whom Big Ben is named.**

★ He was London's Chief Commissioner of Works.

★ Big Ben is the bell not the clock.

DAVID A. HALL

★ **Made a 603-pound haggis; in 1986.**

JOYCE C. HALL 1891-1982

★ **The founder of Hallmark Greeting Cards in 1913.**

ANDREW SMITH HALLIDIE

★ **Engineer who developed San Francisco's cable cars.**

★ The cars went into service on August 1, 1873, on Clay Street Hill.

HANNIBAL HAMLIN 1809-1891

★ **Lincoln's vice-president in his first term; in 1861.**

★ He was a Democratic senator from Maine from 1848 to 1857 but became a Republican over the issue of slavery.

THOMAS HANCOCK 1786-1865

★ **Patented vulcanized rubber in 1843.**

★ He also produced (in 1825) the first toy balloons in Britain.

BARBARA HANDLER

★ **The Barbie doll is named for her.**

★ She is the daughter of the founders of the Mattell Toy Company, Ruth and Elliot Handler; Ken is her brother.

JONAS HANWAY 1712-1786

★ **Made it respectable for a man to carry an umbrella.**

★ At first he was ridiculed as it was thought effeminate; people finally saw it was easier and cheaper than hailing coaches in the rain.

WILLIAM HARBUTT 1844-1921

★ **Created Plasticine; in the late 1800s.**

BEN
HARDAWAY

★ **Cartoonist who did the original sketches for Bugs Bunny.**
★ His nickname was Bugs so they named the character after him.

ROLLA N.
HARGER

★ **In 1938 he invented the breathalyser.**
★ It was called the Drunkometer and was first used in Indianapolis.

JOHN
HARRINGTON 1561-1612

★ **Inventor of the flushing toilet; in 1596.**
★ English courtier and poet who was also Elizabeth I's godson.
★ He installed the first toilet at his house in Bath, England.

THOMAS
HARRIOTT 1560-1621

★ **English scientist who discovered sunspots in 1610.**

JOEL CHANDLER
HARRIS 1848-1908

★ **Black writer who created the "Uncle Remus" character.**
★ First appeared in "Uncle Remus, His Songs and Sayings" in 1880.

RAY
HARROUN 1879-1968

★ **American who won the first Indianapolis 500; in 1911.**
★ The average speed was 74.59 miles per hour; he drove a 6-cylinder Marmon Wasp in 6 hours, 42 minutes, and 8 seconds.

EZEKIEL HART c.1770-1843

★ **First Jew to be elected to a Canadian legislature; in 1807.**
★ He was elected to the Legislative Assembly of Lower Canada twice but would swear his oath only on the Old Testament so he was expelled both times.

JOHN HARWOOD

★ **In 1923, he patented the self-winding watch; in Switzerland.**

EARL HASS

★ **Invented the tampon in 1937.**
★ Modified the surgical tampon, calling it a hygienic tampon; he started the Tampax Company in the same year.

WILLIAM "PUDGE" HEFFELFINGER 1867-1954

★ **First pro football player; in 1892.**
★ He earned $500 for playing for the Allegheny Athletic Association.
★ He was selected to the first college All American Team in 1889.

NEAL HEFTI

★ **He wrote the theme music for TV's "Batman."**

WILLIAM ERNEST HENLEY 1849-1903

★ **The model for Robert Louis Stevenson's Long John Silver.**
★ He also collaborated with Stevenson on four plays.

PAUL
HENNING

★ **The creative genius responsible for "The Beverly Hillbillies," "Petticoat Junction," and "Green Acres."**

JOSIAH (REVEREND)
HENSON 1789-1883

★ **Reputed to be Uncle Tom in *Uncle Tom's Cabin*.**
★ Kentucky slave who escaped to Upper Canada (Ontario) by the Underground Railroad in 1830.

MATTHEW A.
HENSON 1866-1955

★ **Of the six who started, he was the only person to accompany Peary to the North Pole; in 1909.**

HENRY WILLIAM
HERBERT 1807-1858

★ **He was the first American sports writer; in 1839.**

WILLIAM HENRY
HERNDON 1818-1891

★ **Abraham Lincoln's law partner.**

PAUL
HEWSON 1960-

★ **Real name of Bono, lead singer for U2.**

DUBOSE
HEYWARD 1885-1940

★ **Author of the novel *Porgy*, which was turned into a play and then the musical *Porgy and Bess*.**

WILLIAM EDWARD
HICKSON 1803-1870

★ **He coined the cliché "If at first you don't succeed, try, try again."**

MARGUERITE
HIGGINS 1920-1966

★ **The only woman correspondent at the Korean War front.**
★ American journalist who also reported from Vietnam in the 60s.

BREWSTER
HIGLEY

★ **Wrote the poem "Home on the Range"; in 1873.**

MILDRED J.
HILL 1859-1916

★ **With her sister wrote "Happy Birthday"; in 1893.**
★ Her sister was Patty Smith Hill (1868-1946). The second stanza, which became "Happy Birthday," was actually added by the publisher. It is under copyright until 2010.

ROWLAND (SIR)
HILL 1795-1879

★ **Inventor of the prepaid postage stamp; in 1840.**
★ Previously the addressee paid on receipt of the letters, and rates varied according to distance.

JOHN A.
HILLERICH

★ **Produced the first Louisville Slugger baseball bat; in 1884.**
★ He owned a wood-turning business in Louisville, Kentucky. The first bats were custom-made.

JAMES C.
HOBAN 1762-1831

★ **He designed the White House; from 1792 to 1800.**

ELIZABETH
HODGES

★ **She was hit by a meteorite as she napped in 1954.**

★ The meteorite weighed 8.5 pounds and was 7 inches long. It is on display in the University of Alabama's Museum of Natural History.

PETER C. L.
HODGSON 1912-1976

★ **Ad exec who named and marketed Silly Putty in 1950.**

RICHARD MARSH
HOE 1812-1886

★ **Inventor of the rotary printing press; in 1846.**

ELIZABETH PASCHEL
HOISINGTON

★ **The first female general in the U.S. Armed Forces.**

★ Appointed in 1970. She and her brother Peter Milo Hoisington were the first two generals who were brother and sister.

JOHN PHILIP
HOLLAND 1840-1914

★ **Built and launched the first successful submarine; in 1878.**

WEBB PARMALLEE
HOLLENBECK 1891-1966

★ **Real name of actor Clifton Webb.**

RICHARD MILTON
HOLLINGSHEAD

★ **Created the drive-in movie; first one opened June 6, 1933.**
★ He got his start by projecting movies in his driveway.

ELEANOR
HOLM 1913-

★ **Champion swimmer thrown off the 1936 U.S. Olympic team.**
★ Her crime was drinking champagne in public and shooting craps on board the ship to Germany. This punishment appears not to have been a setback for her: she went on to play Jane in a Tarzan movie and to star in aquacades, as well as singing in a band.

EDWIN THOMAS
HOLMES

★ **Installed the first burglar alarm; in 1858 in Boston.**
★ In 1877 he invented a switchboard/burglar alarm. By day it was a telephone system and at night it was a burglar alarm.

ROBERT
HORN

★ **He preceded Dick Clark as host of "American Bandstand"; from 1952 to 1956.**

H. RICHARD
HORNBERGER

★ **Wrote the novel *M*A*S*H* on which the movie was based.**
★ American physician who had served in a MASH unit in Korea.

FRANK
HORNBY D. 1936

★ **He invented Meccano; in 1901.**

JOHN CALCOTT HORSLEY 1817-1903

★ **Designed the first "commercial" Christmas card; in 1843.**

DAVID HOSACK 1769-1835

★ **Physician who was founder of Bellevue Hospital.**

★ He also attended Alexander Hamilton after his duel with Aaron Burr.

ROSE LOUISE HOVICK 1914-1970

★ **Otherwise known as stripper Gypsy Rose Lee.**

JACK HOWARTH

★ **Actor who played Uncle Albert Tatlock for 23 years on "Coronation Street."**

WILLIAM DE HART HUBBARD 1903-1976

★ **He was the first black American to win an Olympic gold medal in an individual event; in the long jump in 1924.**

THOMAS STERRY HUNT 1826-1892

★ **Invented the green ink used for printing U.S. paper money.**

★ Hunt was an American teaching at McGill. The ink has been used since 1862; its success was due to its inability to be photographically imitated, foiling counterfeiters. His invention is responsible for the nickname for U.S. bills — "greenbacks."

HERMAN HUPFELD

★ **Wrote the song "As Time Goes By"; in 1931.**

★ He also wrote "When Yuba Plays the Rumba on His Tuba."

DORIS AND FRANK HURLEY

★ **Creators of the daytime soap "General Hospital"; in 1963.**

WILLIAM HUSKISSON 1770-1830

★ **He was the first railway fatality; in 1830.**

★ British politican who was killed crossing the tracks at the official opening of the Manchester-Liverpool line. He was on his way to greet the prime minister and the Duke of Wellington. This was the first accident caused by a moving train; two earlier fatalities were railway employees killed on the job.

CHRISTIAAN HUYGENS 1629-1695

★ **Built the first pendulum clock; in 1656.**

★ He also discovered the rings of Saturn and propounded the first wave theory of light.

JOHN WESLEY HYATT 1837-1920

★ **Inventor of celluloid (and named it); in 1870.**

★ He invented it in response to a manufacturer of ivory billiard balls who wanted an inexpensive substitute for ivory. He also invented a water filter; multiple-needle sewing machine; a knife sharpener.

★ Alexander Parkes discovered the same substance but never made it a success.

YVES-GÉRARD ILLOUZ

- ★ **He is a French doctor who perfected the technique of liposuction in 1977.**

JAN INGENHOUSZ 1730-1799

- ★ **He discovered photosynthesis in 1779.**
- ★ Dutch physician and plant physiologist.
- ★ He was also physician to Empress Maria Theresa.

MAY IRWIN 1862-1934

- ★ **First actress in a commercial film to share a kiss; in 1896.**
- ★ The one-minute movie was "The Kiss." It scandalised the audience, leading to the first demands for screen censorship.
- ★ Her co-star co-kisser was John Rice.

CHARLES ISHAM 1819-1903

- ★ **Put the first known garden gnome in his garden in 1847.**
- ★ This British eccentric believed the garden gnomes, which he placed in his rockery, were real people.

ALEC CONSTANTINE ISSIGONIS 1906-1988

- ★ **Added the word "mini" to the English vocabulary by designing the Mini in 1959.**
- ★ He had designed the Morris Minor car in 1948; it was produced until 1971.
- ★ He was an engineer who was born in Turkey but settled in Britain in 1923.

ANNE MARIE LOUISA ITALIANO 1931-

★ **Real name of actress Anne Bancroft.**

DMITRILOSIFOVICH IVANOVSKY

★ **Russian microbiologist who discovered the first virus in 1892.**

★ The virus was the cause of the tobacco mosaic, a disease that attacks a variety of plants.

UBBE IWERKS 1901-1971

★ **Designed and developed Mickey Mouse; in 1927.**

★ He was an early collaborator of Walt Disney. In 1920 they created the Disney-Iwerks Studio.

★ His first film was "Plane Crazy" (1928) starring Mickey Mouse. He was also a director of Porky Pig cartoons. He won Academy Awards for technical achievement in 1959 and 1964.

SHIGECHIYO IZUMI 1865-1986

★ **Lived to be 120 years, 237 days old.**

★ He died of pneumonia.

ELLIE AND RAYMOND JACOBS

★ **They brought Earth shoes to the United States.**

★ Brought from Copenhagen; designed there by Anne Kalso.

MARY PHELPS JACOBS

★ **Designed the first brassiere; patented in 1914.**

★ She made the first one with two white handkerchiefs, a strand of ribbon, and some cord. She eventually sold the patent to Warner Brothers Corset Company for $15,000.

RICHARD JACQUET D.1686

★ **England's executioner from 1678 to 1686.**

ANTHONY JANNUS

★ **Pilot of the first scheduled airline flight – between Tampa and St. Petersburg.**

ANNA JARVIS 1864-1948

★ **Started Mother's Day; in 1908 in Grafton, West Virginia.**

CHRISTO VLADIMIROV JAVACHEFF 1935-

★ **Bulgarian artist who wraps figures, buildings, etc. in fabric (usually white).**

★ Some of the items that he has wrapped: part of the Australian coastline and Clint Eastwood.

WILLIAM LE BARON JENNEY 1832-1907

★ **Designer of the first "skyscraper."**

★ It was the 10-storey Home Insurance Co. Building in Chicago, completed in 1885.

JENS KJAER JENSION 1914-

★ **He had 32,131 thorns removed from his body after he fell into a prickly bush.**

★ It took 248 visits spread over six years to remove them.

ALFRED JODL 1890-1946

★ **The German general who signed the surrender of the German Armed Forces on May 7, 1945.**

★ He was tried for war crimes in Nuremberg in 1945 and hanged.

OPHA MAY JOHNSON

★ **The first woman to join the U.S. Marine Corps; in 1918.**

TOM LOFTIN JOHNSON 1854-1911

★ **Invented the transparent fare box; in 1873.**

JEAN BAPTISTE JOLLY

★ **Established the first dry-cleaners; in Paris, in 1855.**

★ He accidentally discovered the principle of dry cleaning when he spilled some turpentine on a dress; it didn't stain, but cleaned!

HAROLD SPENCER (SIR) JONES — 1890-1960

★ **Determined the distance between the sun and the earth.**

★ British astronomer; Astronomer Royal from 1933 to 1955.

★ It took him 12 years to make the calculation.

JOSEF JONSSEN

★ **Invented aluminum foil bottle caps; in 1915.**

ANATOL MARCO JOSEPHO

★ **Hungarian who invented the photo booth; in 1950.**

★ First booths had attendants; were replaced by a coin slot in 1968.

WILLIAM JOYCE — 1906-1946

★ **He was known as Lord Haw-Haw.**

★ He was born in Brooklyn but moved to Ireland as a child. During World War II, he broadcast for the Germans. He was hanged for treason. His upper-class accent gave rise to the nickname.

ROBERT AND JEAN JUDET

★ **Frenchmen who performed first human bone graft in 1950.**

WHITCOMB L. JUDSON

★ **Patented the first zipper; in 1896.**

★ First design had many imperfections. In 1913, a Swede in New Jersey improved it. In 1905 Automatic Hook and Eye Co. began making modern zippers, under brand name of C-Curity.

K

HERBERT THOMAS
KALMUS 1881-1963

★ **Invented Technicolor; in 1912.**
★ Made the first Technicolor one-reeler in 1917. Team members were D.F. Comstock and W.B. Westcott.

BOB
KANE 1916-

★ **Creator of Batman.**
★ The superhero was created for "Detective Comics" in 1939.

HELEN
KANE 1904-1966

★ **Singer on whom the cartoon character Betty Boop is based.**
★ She was known as the Boop-a-Doop Girl.

JIGORO
KANO 1860-1938

★ **Japanese professor who invented judo; in 1882.**
★ He combined principles of different forms of ju-jitsu.

STEFAN GEIR
KARLSSON

★ **Icelander who built the world's largest coathanger.**
★ It weighs 440 pounds, measures 15 feet by 6.75 feet by 1.6 feet, and is made of pine and plywood.

ALPHONSE
KARR 1808-1890

★ **French journalist and novelist who wrote "The more things change, the more they stay the same"; in 1849.**

ANNETTE KELLERMAN

★ **First nude appearance in a motion picture; in 1916.**

★ In 1907 was the first woman to wear a one-piece bathing suit; also first woman to try to swim the English Channel; her life story was made into "Million-Dollar Mermaid," starring Esther Williams.

PERT KELTON

★ **She played Alice Kramden in the first appearance of "The Honeymooners."**

★ The first show was a sketch on "Calvacade of Stars" in 1951.

WILLIAM KEMMLER 1862-1890

★ **Axe murderer who was first man to die in the electric chair; in 1890 in Auburn State Prison, N.Y.**

WILLIAM KEMP

★ **Morris-danced from London to Norwich in nine days; in 1599.**

HERBERT BUCKINGHAM KHAURY 1930-

★ **Real name of entertainer and ukulele player Tiny Tim.**

HAR GOBIND KHORANA 1922-

★ **Scientist who led the team that produced the first biologically active artificial gene; in 1976.**

LAURA
KIELER

★ **Ibsen used her as a model for Nora in *A Doll's House*.**

JAKE
KILRAIN 1859-1937

★ **Was the loser in the last bare-knuckle championship fight.**
★ He lost to John L. Sullivan in a match that lasted 75 rounds in 1889.

HUSBAND EDWARD
KIMMEL 1882-1964

★ **Commander of the Pearl Harbor naval base at the time of the Japanese attack in 1941.**

LESLIE
KING, JR. 1913-

★ **Real name of former U.S. president Gerald R. Ford.**

GUSTAV ROBERT
KIRCHHOFF 1824-1887

★ **Invented the spectroscope; in 1859.**
★ The spectroscope can study atoms and molecules in a gaseous or liquid phase.

MAX
KISS 1883-1967

★ **Developed Ex-lax in 1906.**
★ Hungarian pharmacist who combined chocolate with laxatives. The name stands for Excellent Laxative.

SHIBASABURO KITASATO 1852-1931

★ **Discovered bacterium causing bubonic plague; in 1894.**
★ Japanese physician.

PHILIP KIVES 1929-

★ **Canadian founder of the K-tel company.**
★ The company was noted for its consumer products such as the Veg-O-Matic food slicer and the Miracle Brush lint remover.

ISIDORE KLEIN

★ **Animator who drew Mighty Mouse.**
★ He also drew the character Little Audrey.

RICHARD P. KNERR / ARTHUR K. "SPUD" MELVIN

★ **Invented the hula-hoop; in 1958.**
★ They also trademarked the word Frisbee in 1959.

ROBERT KOLDEWEY 1855-1925

★ **Discovered Babylon, thought to be a myth; in 1898.**
★ German archaeologist who also discovered the foundations of the Tower of Babel.

WILLEM JOHANN KOLFF 1911-

★ **Developed the artificial kidney dialysis machine.**
★ He treated the first patient with it in 1943.

CARL
KOLLER 1857-1944

★ **Discovered cocaine as a pain-killer; in 1884.**

★ Cocaine was already known but Koller introduced it as a local anaesthesia. He experimented on animals and on himself.

JYRKI RISTO
KORHONEN ANTIKAINEN

★ **Threw an egg a record-breaking 317 feet and 10 inches between the two of them; in Finland in 1981.**

RICHARD VON
KRAFFT-EBING 1840-1902

★ **Coined the words paranoia, sadism, masochism.**

★ German psychiatrist who introduced these terms in his study of sexual deviation *Psychopathia Sexualis* in 1886.

RICK
KRAUSE

★ **Spit a cherry pit 72 feet, 7.5 inches; in 1988 in Michigan.**

JOSEPH
KRIEGER

★ **First to put tea in bags; in 1920 in San Francisco.**

★ Originally the bags were used only by caterers, but by 1935 most were used in the home.

ROMAN IVAN GRAEME ROBERT
KROITOR FERGUSON KERR

★ **Developed IMAX; in 1967.**

★ IMAX cinemas have screens six stories high and 80 feet wide. It stands for eye (I) and maximum (MAX), the most the eye can see.

BENJAMIN
KUBELSKY 1894-1974

★ **Real name of Jack Benny.**

MARGARET
KUHN 1905-

★ **One of the organizers of the Gray Panthers; in 1970.**
★ Their rallying cry is "Out of the rocking chair, into the street!"

RÜDOLF
KUHNOLD

★ **Developer of radar; first demonstrated in 1934.**

JUGALCHANDRA
KUNDU

★ **Wrote a poem of 437 characters on one grain of rice; in 1989.**

DAVID
KUNST 1939-

★ **American who was the first person to walk around the world.**
★ He left Waseca, Minnesota, on June 20, 1970, and arrived back on October 5, 1974.

IGOR VASILEVITCH
KURCHATOV 1903-1960

★ **Led the groups that developed the A-bomb (1949) and H-bomb (1952) in the U.S.S.R.**

THOMAS E. **JOHN G.**
KURTZ **KEMENY**

★ **Inventors of the computer language BASIC; in 1964.**

CHERILYN SARKISIAN
LA PIERRE 1946-

★ **Real name of Cher.**

★ In a survey of American high school students, some thought that Chernobyl was Cher's real name.

RUDOLPH
LABAN 1879-1958

★ **Invented the notation system for a graphic shorthand for dance movements; in 1928.**

★ He called it "Labanotation."

RENÉ THÉOPHILE HYACINTHE
LAËNNEC 1781-1826

★ **French army doctor who invented the stethoscope; in 1814.**

SELMA
LAGERLOF 1858-1940

★ **First woman to win the Nobel Prize in Literature; in 1909.**

JOSEPH LOUIS
LAGRANGE 1736-1813

★ **Chaired the commission that introduced the metric system; in 1793.**

JEAN BAPTISTE PIERRE ANTOINE DE
LAMARCK 1774-1829

★ **French zoologist who created the terms vertebrate and invertebrate.**

★ He developed an early theory of evolution (Lamarckism) that said that changes acquired in an individual's lifetime are passed on to future generations.

EDWIN HENRY
LANDSEER 1802-1873

★ **Designed the lions at the base of the Nelson Monument in Trafalgar Square, London.**

KARL
LANDSTEINER 1868-1943

★ **In 1900-02 discovered and classified the four major blood groups, A, B, AB, and O.**

★ Austrian pathologist who aided in the discovery of the Rh factor in 1940 and made contributions to the treatment of polio.

ALLAN "ROCKY"
LANE

★ **Voice of Mr. Ed.**

LUPINO
LANE D.1959

★ **He introduced the Lambeth Walk in 1937.**

★ The dance consisted of pairs strutting forward, arms linked, then strutting back, jerking their thumbs in the air and exclaiming "Oy!" It was an intense and short-lived dance fad in 1938 in Britain and the United States.

MURRAY
LANGSTON

★ **Played the Unknown Comic on "The Gong Show."**

DOMINIQUE JEAN
LARREY 1766-1842

★ **Created the first ambulance service; in 1792.**

★ He was Napoleon's personal surgeon from 1797.

JOHN A. LARSON

★ **In 1921 he invented the lie detector.**

★ He was a medical student when he invented it.

EUGENE AUGUSTIN LAUSTE 1856-1935

★ **He created the first sound on motion picture film and patented the process in 1906.**

CALIXA LAVALLÉE 1842-1891

★ **Wrote the music for "O Canada."**

★ First sung in public in Quebec City in 1880; adopted as the national anthem in 1980. French words were by Adolphe Basile Routhier; English words were by Robert Stanley Weir.

CHARLES LOUIS ALPHONSE LAVERAN 1845-1922

★ **He was a French physician who in 1880 put forth the theory that malaria was spread by mosquitoes.**

JOHN BENNET LAWES 1814-1899

★ **Pioneer in synthetic fertilizers; in 1839.**

★ The first synthetic fertilizer was used on turnip crops.

OLIVIER LE JEUNE D.1654

★ **The first black to be recorded as a slave in Canada; in 1632.**

★ He's actually registered as a servant because slavery was illegal at the time. He came from Madagascar.

LOUIS
LE VAU 1612-1670

★ **The architect and builder of Versailles; from 1661.**
★ Aided by André Lenôtre; built the Louvre and Les Tuileries.

DOUGLAS
LEIGH 1907-

★ **Responsible for first neon signs in Times Square; in 1937.**
★ The first sign was a Coca-Cola weather sign (1937). Another was the Camel cigarettes' smoking man (1941).

ANNA
LEONOWENS

★ **She is the governess who is Anna in "The King and I."**

MARC
LESCARBOT

★ **Founded the first public library in the western hemisphere; in 1606 at Port Royal, Nova Scotia.**
★ He loaned books from his own collection.

ROBERT GILMOUR
LETOURNEAU 1888-1969

★ **In 1926 he invented the bulldozer.**
★ He was an earth-mover who put a steel scraper blade in front of a tractor and equipped it with an electric cable.

MILTON
LEVINE

★ **Started selling mail-order Ant Farms; in 1956.**
★ The ants are bought separately from the farm; the buyer gets a certificate to exchange for the ants when ready to start.

RICHARD LEVINSON / **WILLIAM LINK**

★ **Creators of the rumpled TV detective Columbo.**

WILLARD FRANK LIBBY 1908-1980

★ **Developed radio-carbon dating in 1947.**

★ Radio-carbon dating determines the age of organic or fossilized material from its radioactive carbon content.

RALPH LIFSHITZ

★ **Real name of designer Ralph Lauren.**

LYDIA KAMEKEHA LILUOKALANI 1838-1917

★ **Last Hawaiian queen to rule before the annexation of the islands to the United States; from 1891 to 1893.**

★ She also composed "Aloha Oe" in 1879.

JAMES LIND 1716-1794

★ **Discovered that lemons prevented scurvy; in 1747.**

KATHLEEN LINDSAY 1903-1973

★ **South African who wrote 904 novels in her lifetime.**

ARTHUR B. LINTGEN 1932-

★ **Can identify the music on a phonograph disc simply by examining the record. He does not have to hear it played.**

ALEXANDER
LION

★ **Doctor who devised the premature baby incubator; in 1891.**
★ In its first three years, 137 out of 185 preemies survived infancy, something unlikely to have happened without the incubator.

HYMAN
LIPMAN

★ **Patented a pencil with an eraser attached to one end; in 1858.**

HANS
LIPPERSHEY c.1570-c.1619

★ **Dutch lens and spectacle maker who demonstrated the first telescope in 1608.**

ROBERT R.
LIVINGSTONE 1746-1813

★ **He administered the oath of office to Washington in 1789.**
★ He was also the first secretary of state and one of five men charged with drawing up the Declaration of Independence.

JOSEPH L.
LOCKARD

★ **Radar operator at Pearl Harbor who spotted approaching Japanese planes, but thought they were friendly aircraft.**

BELVA ANN
LOCKWOOD 1830-1917

★ **She was the first woman candidate for U.S. president.**
★ She ran against Grover Cleveland as candidate of the Equal Rights Party in 1884 and 1888; also the first woman to practise before the Supreme Court.

MILTON B.
LOEB 1887-1972

★ **Created Brillo cleaning pads.**

CRAWFORD WILLIAMSON
LONG 1815-1878

★ **First to use ether as an anaesthetic; in Georgia, in 1842.**
★ He removed a cyst from the neck of a student. The operation took place in 1842, but he didn't reveal he had done it until 1849.

MICHAEL
LOOKINLAND

★ **Actor who played Bobby Brady on "The Brady Bunch."**

MAHLON
LOOMIS 1826-1886

★ **Holds the first patent for radio; in 1872 in the United States.**
★ It was called "Improvement in Telegraphy."

GRISWOLD
LORILLARD

★ **He wore the first tuxedo in 1886.**
★ It was modelled on the English smoking jacket. He first wore it to a ball at the Tuxedo Park Country Club, New York.

MICHEL
LOTITO 1950-

★ **Frenchman who eats as much as two pounds of metal a day.**
★ Since 1966, he has eaten such metal and non-metal items as bicycles, a shopping cart, TV sets, chandeliers, a Cessna light aircraft, and a coffin.

ANTOINE
LOUIS

★ **He was the designer of the guillotine and was killed by it.**

★ Co-designer was Tobias Schmidt, a harpsichord maker; Louis was a surgeon. First victim was Nicolas Jacques Pelletier.

JAMES SPENCER
LOVE 1896-1962

★ **In 1924 he became the first manufacturer of rayon.**

★ He had founded Burlington Industries in 1923.

JULIETTE GORDON
LOW 1860-1927

★ **Founder of Girl Guides of America in 1912.**

★ It was renamed Girl Scouts in 1913.

HUDSON
LOWE 1766-1842

★ **As governor of St. Helena, he was Napoleon's jailer from 1816 to 1821.**

HUGH
LYGON 1904-1936

★ **Evelyn Waugh based Sebastian Flyte on him in *Brideshead Revisited*.**

MARY
LYON 1797-1849

★ **Founded first women's college in the United States; in 1837.**

★ It was Mt. Holyoke College and started with 80 students. It was the first non-profit women's college in the United States.

JOHN
MACARTHUR 1767-1834

★ **In 1797, he introduced merino sheep to Australia.**
★ He also established the first commercial vineyard in Australia.

COLIN **MACFARQUHAR**
ANDREW **BELL**

★ **Started the *Encyclopedia Britannica*; in Edinburgh in 1768.**
★ Macfarquhar was a printer and bookseller and Bell was an engraver, reputedly of dog collars.

JOHN JAMES RICKARD
MACLEOD 1876-1935

★ **Shared the Nobel Prize with F.G. Banting for his work on the use of insulin for treating diabetes; in 1923.**

KIRKPATRICK
MACMILLAN 1813-1878

★ **Invented the first bicycle that could be pedalled; in 1839.**
★ Scottish blacksmith; he never patented it and it was widely copied; he got the idea while trying to figure out how to get a hobbyhorse to move.

LELAND "LARRY" STANFORD
MACPHAIL 1890-1975

★ **Introduced night games to baseball.**
★ He died October 1, 1975, at the age of 85.

EDWARD
MADDRELL 1877-1974

★ **He was the last man whose official tongue was Manx.**

JOHANNN NEPOMUK
MAELZEL 1722-1838

★ **Austrian physician who patented the metronome; in 1816.**

CARLTON C.
MAGEE 1873-1946

★ **American newspaper editor who invented the parking meter.**
★ They were first installed in Oklahoma City in 1935.

FRANCIS
MAKEMIE 1658-1708

★ **He was an American clergyman who is regarded as the founder of presbyterianism.**

MARY
MALLON 1855-1938

★ **Real name of Typhoid Mary.**
★ Also known as Maria Anna Caduff, she was an itinerant cook who carried the salmonella microbe that causes typhoid.

ALDUS
MANUTIUS 1450-1515

★ **Produced the world's first paperbacks.**
★ Italian editor and printer who was also the first to print books in Greek. He also introduced italics.

WALTER
MAP 1140-1209

★ **It is believed he wrote down the story of Launcelot, which was used in later accounts of the Arthurian legends.**
★ Welsh cleric and satirist.

ITALO
MARCIONI

★ **Patented ice cream cones; in 1903 in New York.**

★ He invented the moulds in 1896.

ENID
MARKEY 1890-1981

★ **Acress who played Jane in the first Tarzan movies.**

★ The first movies were "Tarzan of the Apes" and "The Romance of Tarzan." Both were made in 1918 with Elmo Leonard as Tarzan.

JOHN D.
MARKS

★ **Wrote the song "Rudolph the Red-Nosed Reindeer."**

FREDERICK
MARRYAT 1792-1848

★ **He wrote "There's no getting blood out of a turnip."**

JAMES WILSON
MARSHALL 1810-1885

★ **Discovered gold at Sutter's Mill, Colorado; in 1848.**

ABRAHAM
MARTIN

★ **Owned the property on which the Battle of the Plains of Abraham was fought.**

★ The battle was fought in 1759. General Wolfe led 4500 British soldiers up a steep cliff that led to the plains. Wolfe and Montcalm, the latter leading the French forces, were both killed in the battle.

★ The land had been granted to Martin between 1635 and 1645.

CLARA BRETT MARTIN 1874-1923

★ **She was the first female lawyer in the British Empire; in 1897.**

LOCK MARTIN

★ **Actor who played the robot Gort in "The Day the Earth Stood Still"; in 1957.**

★ He had been the doorman at Graumann's Chinese Theater.

MELISSA MATHISON

★ **She was the screenwriter for the movie "E.T."**

BERNARD MATTHEWS

★ **Turkey farm owner with 8.5 million turkeys.**

REUBEN MATTUS

★ **He developed and marketed Häagen-Dazs ice cream.**

BILLY AND BOBBY MAUCH 1925-

★ **Twin actors who appeared in "The Prince and the Pauper"; with Errol Flynn in 1937.**

DAVID L. MAUND

★ **Has a collection of over 7,000 miniature Scotch whiskey bottles.**

MAURY
MAVERICK

★ **Coined the word gobbledygook; in 1944.**

★ He said he got his inspiration for the word, which he used to describe bureaucratic jargon, from the gobblings of turkeys.

HIRAM STEVENS
MAXIM 1840-1916

★ **Invented the automatic machine gun; in 1884.**

★ The gun was the first continuous-firing automatic machine gun. The basic principle of the gun he invented is still used today in most machine guns.

KITTY
MAXSE 1867-1922

★ **Virginia Woolf based Mrs. Dalloway on her in the novel of the same name.**

WILHELM
MAYBACH 1846-1929

★ **Rode the first motorcycle; in 1885.**

★ It reached a speed of 12 miles per hour.

JOHN B.
MAYENBERG

★ **Patented unsweetened evaporated milk in 1884.**

HENRY
McCARTY 1859-1881

★ **Real name of Billy the Kid.**

★ He changed his name to William Bonney when he was teenager.

ROBERT JOHN LE MESURIER McCLURE 1807-1873

★ **He proved the existence of the Northwest Passage.**

★ The search for the Northwest Passage began in the 15th century but it wasn't until his explorations of 1850 to 1854 that he found it. Its discovery is usually credited to John Franklin.

ELMER VERNER McCOLLUM 1879-1967

★ **Originated the letter system for naming vitamins.**

DAVID J. McCONNELL

★ **Founder of Avon Products.**

★ He was a door-to-door salesman who gave away small bottles of cologne to encourage the purchase of his books. The cologne was more popular than the books so in 1886 he began to make perfumes. He hired women to sell the products door to door.

CYRUS HALL McCORMICK 1809-1884

★ **He invented the reaper machine and patented it in 1834.**

★ He started the company that became International Harvester.

PATRICIA McCORMICK

★ **She was the first American woman bullfighter.**

★ She was from Texas and made her pro debut in 1952, in Mexico.

JOHNSTON McCULLEY

★ **Creator of Zorro; in 1919.**

ROBERT
McCULLOCH 1911-1977

★ **Bought London Bridge and moved it to Arizona; in 1968.**

ELIAS
McDANIEL 1928-

★ **Real name of musician Bo Diddley.**

RICHARD "TERRY"
McDERMOTT 1940-

★ **He is the speedskater who won the only gold medal for the United States in the 1964 Winter Olympics.**

HUGH C.
McDONALD

★ **Put together the first Identikit for identifying criminals.**
★ He dissected 50,000 photos and made them into 500 "master foils." A kit had 37 noses, 52 chins, 102 pairs of eyes, 40 lips, 130 hairlines, and an assortment of eyebrows, beards, moustaches, spectacles, wrinkles and headgear.

PETER J.
McGUIRE

★ **Conceived of idea of Labor Day; signed into law in 1894.**
★ President of United Brotherhood of Carpenters and Joiners of America. It was first celebrated in 1882 in New York City.

FRANK
McGURRIN

★ **He was the first touch typist.**
★ He demonstrated the skill at a speed typing contest in 1888 (he won it).

THOMAS McKEAN 1734-1817

★ **Last man to sign the Declaration of Independence; five years after everyone else, in 1781.**

GRAHAM McNAMEE 1888-1942

★ **Commentator of the first broadcast baseball game; in 1929.**
★ It was the World Series, from the Polo Grounds; he also broadcast the first Rose Bowl to be heard from coast to coast.

HERMAN CYRIL McNEILE 1888-1937

★ **Creator of the Bulldog Drummond character.**

NORRIS AND ROSS McWHIRTER

★ **British twins who wrote and published the first *Guinness Book of Records*; in 1955.**
★ Born in 1925. Ross was killed in 1975 in an IRA terrorist attack.

HIPPOLYTE MÈGE-MOURIÉS 1817-1880

★ **He patented margarine in Paris in 1869.**
★ His first efforts, which were tallow-based, were quite unappetising but nevertheless won a prize from the French government. Adding emulsified skim milk improved the texture.

ANDREW MEIKLE 1719-1811

★ **Scottish engineer who invented the threshing machine in 1786.**

JOSEPH
MEISTER 1876-1940

★ **He was the nine-year-old boy who in 1885 was the first patient given the rabies vaccine by Louis Pasteur.**
★ As an adult, he was the conciérge of the Pasteur Institute and committed suicide rather than open Pasteur's tomb for the Nazis.

KEVIN
MELLISH 1948-

★ **This bargain-hunter stood in line for 20 days in 1986 to buy a carpet that was reduced in price by 86%.**

OTTMAR
MERGENTHALER 1854-1899

★ **Invented the linotype machine; in 1886.**
★ It cast metal type in complete lines instead of individual letters. The first 30 machines were installed at the New York *Tribune*.

PROSPER
MÉRIMÉE 1803-1870

★ **Wrote "Carmen," the source of Bizet's opera.**

JOSEPH
MERLIN

★ **Wore the first known pair of roller skates; in 1760.**
★ Belgian instrument maker; rolled into a fashionable masquerade party as he played a violin and crashed into a mirror.

CAROL
MERRILL

★ **One of the models on "Let's Make a Deal" from 1963 to 1976.**

FLEURY
MESPLET
1734-1794

★ **Published first French newspaper in North America; in 1778.**

★ It was *La Gazette de commerce et littéraire*, published in Montreal.

OTTO
MESSMER
1894-1985

★ **Creator of Felix the Cat.**

★ Although Pat Sullivan (1887-1933) drew the first Felix, the final and best known Felix was put together by Messmer.

ALBERT ABRAHAM
MICHELSON
1852-1931

★ **He refined the measurement of the speed of light in 1882.**

★ He was the first American scientist to win the Nobel Prize in Physics (1907). His interfermometer made possible the most accurate measurement of light for the next 50 years.

MORRIS
MICHTOM

★ **He made the first teddy bear; in 1902.**

★ He named the bear after Teddy Roosevelt. In 1903 he started Ideal Toy.

CHARLES VANCE
MILLAR
1853-1926

★ **Canadian bachelor who left the bulk of his estate for a stork derby; in 1938.**

★ He stipulated that the money should go to the Toronto mother who gave birth to the most children in the 10 years following his death. It was ultimately shared among four women, one of whom was Lucy Alice Timeleck, mother of 18 children.

WILLIAM MILLER 1810-1872

★ **Scottish poet who wrote the poem "Wee Willie Winkie."**
★ He was a woodturner by profession.

FERENC MOLNÁR 1878-1952

★ **Hungarian who wrote the play that *Carousel* is based on.**
★ The play is called *Liliom* and was written in 1909.

ARTHUR R. MOMAND

★ **Coined the phrase "Keeping Up With the Joneses."**
★ His comic strip with that title started in 1913 and ran for 28 years.

GIOVANNI BATTISTA MONTINI 1897-1978

★ **This was the real name of Pope Paul VI.**
★ He was pope from June 21, 1963, to August 6, 1978.

CLEMENT CLARK MOORE 1779-1863

★ **In 1822, he wrote "Twas the Night Before Christmas."**
★ He called it "A Visit from St. Nicholas" and it was first published in the *Troy Sentinel* on December 23, 1823.

THOMAS HUNT MORGAN 1866-1945

★ **Originated the gene theory by studying fruit flies.**
★ The theory established the relation between genes and chromosomes, which accounted for the mechanism of heredity.

WILLIAM G.
MORGAN

★ **Invented volleyball in 1895.**
★ It was first called Mintonette and was intended for middle-aged men who couldn't play basketball.

JOHN
MORRELL

★ **Canadian writer who created Rambo.**

BRET
MORRISON 1912-1978

★ **Announcer who introduced The Shadow with "Who knows what evil lurks in the hearts of men? The Shadow knows."**
★ The program was broadcast from 1944 to 1956.

ROBERT
MORRISON 1782-1834

★ **He was the first English missionary to go to China (in 1807).**
★ He also translated the Bible into Chinese.

WILLIAM THOMAS GREEN
MORTON 1819-1868

★ **American dentist who was the first to successfully use an anaesthetic (ether); in Boston in 1846.**
★ The operation was to remove a tumour from a young man's jaw.

SAMUEL ALEXANDER
MUDD

★ **Treated John Wilkes Booth after Lincoln's assassination.**
★ He was charged as a conspirator because he didn't report his patient, was found guilty, and served three and a half years.

PATIENCE
MUFFETT

★ **Child who was the Little Miss Muffett of the nursery rhyme.**

★ Her father, Dr. Thomas Muffet, was an authority on spiders. Truly.

FREDERICK AUGUSTUS CONRAD
MUHLENBERG 1750-1801

★ **First Speaker of the House (1789-97).**

CLARENCE EDWARD
MULFORD 1883-1956

★ **Writer who created Hopalong Cassidy in 1907.**

★ The first story Hopalong appeared in was "Bar 20." He was the hero of novels published from 1910 to 1950. Mulford went west only once and although he hated it, he wrote more than 100 Western novels.

DAVID
MULLANY

★ **In 1955 he created the Wiffle Ball.**

★ The ball is lightweight and has specially cut-out holes to make it curve when it is thrown.

PAUL HERMANN
MULLER 1899-1965

★ **In 1939 he formulated the synthetic insecticide DDT.**

WILLIAM
MURDOCK 1754-1839

★ **Scottish engineer who first used coal-gas lighting; in 1792.**

★ He used it in houses in Redruth in Cornwall, England.

OSAMI NAGANO 1880-1947

★ **The Japanese admiral who planned and ordered the attack on Pearl Harbor.**

JAMES A. NAISMITH 1861-1939

★ **Invented modern basketball; in 1891.**

★ Canadian physical education teacher who taught at a YMCA in Massachusetts.

YOSHIRO NAKAMATA

★ **Japanese inventor of the floppy disk; in 1950.**

★ This multi-talented inventor has patents on such varied items as golf clubs and loudspeakers.

ALAN NAPIER 1903-1988

★ **Actor who played the butler on the TV series "Batman."**

JOHN NAPIER 1550-1617

★ **Invented logarithms and introduced the decimal point.**

★ He also invented Napier's Bones, a mechanical calculating device for multiplication and division and coined the word "logarithms."

CLARENCE NASH 1905-1985

★ **The voice of Donald Duck for 50 years.**

N

THOMAS
NAST 1840-1902

★ **American illustrator who created the Democratic party's donkey and the Republican elephant.**

MYRON
NATWICK 1890-1990

★ **The creator of Betty Boop.**
★ She was the first cartoon character to be censored.

EDWARD A.
NEDELCOV

★ **Has collected 1,131 versions of the spelling of his surname.**
★ He began collecting these misspellings in 1960.

ALEXANDER
NEVERMIND 1960-

★ **Pseudonym used by pop musician Prince, under which he has written and produced for other artists.**
★ Birth name is Prince Rogers Nelson.

PAULA
NEWBY-FRASER 1962-

★ **Five-time winner of the female division of the Ironman Championship.**

NELSON
NEWCOMBE

★ **Designed the Nitelite ball, a golf ball that glows in the dark.**
★ He has designed other glow-in-the-dark sports products such as Frisbees and footballs.

MARY ANNE
NICHOLLS 1846-1888

★ **She was the first victim of Jack the Ripper.**

JEAN SLUTSKY
NIDETCH 1923-

★ **She founded Weight Watchers in 1961.**

JOSEPH NICÉPHORE
NIÉPCE 1765-1833

★ **Produced the first photograph, on pewter plates; in 1826.**
★ Needed an 8-hour exposure; is the earliest surviving photograph.

GEORGE
NISSEN

★ **American inventor of the trampoline; in 1936.**

SILAS
NOBLE

JAMES P.
COOLEY

★ **Inventors of a machine to make toothpicks; in 1872.**

SUZANNE
NOEL D.1954

★ **French surgeon who performed the first facelifts; in 1925.**
★ In the 1930s she practised from her large apartment near the Champs Elysées working with many celebrities. She herself had a number of facelifts in her later years.

TENZIG
NORGAY

★ **Sherpa who accompanied Hilary to top of Everest; in 1953.**

WILLIS HAROLD
O'BRIEN 1886-1962

★ **Special effects man who animated King Kong; in 1933.**
★ He pioneered the use of pliable miniature clay figures.

SEAN ALOYSIUS
O'FEARNA 1895-1973

★ **Real name of American director John Ford.**

GEORGE
O'HANLON 1913-1989

★ **The voice of George Jetson.**

ROSE CECIL
O'NEILL 1874-1944

★ **She originated and designed kewpie dolls; in 1909.**

FREDERICK
OAKLEY 1802-1880

★ **He translated "Adeste Fideles" into English as "O Come, All Ye Faithful" in 1852.**
★ The original words and music were by John Francis Wade.

AMEDEO **MARIO**
OBICI **PERUZZI**

★ **Established Planters Nut and Chocolate Company; in 1907.**

ARCH
OBOLER 1909-

★ **He wrote, produced, and directed the first feature film in 3-D "Bwana Devil"; in 1953.**

CONSTANCE FRANCES MARIE OCKLEMAN 1919-1973

★ **Real name of actress Veronica Lake.**

JAMES EDWARD OGLETHORPE 1696-1785

★ **Englishman who founded the colony of Georgia in 1732.**
★ It was intended as a refuge for debtors and European Protestants.

BERNA "BARNEY" ELI OLDFIELD 1878-1946

★ **First to travel at a mile-a-minute; in 1903.**
★ American who won his first car race only two weeks after learning how to drive a car.

EMILIO ONRA

★ **The first human cannonball; in 1875 in Paris.**

NORMAN ORENTREICH

★ **Doctor who invented the hair transplant in 1959.**
★ He took the hairs from the back of the scalp and transplanted them into the bald spots.

RAYMOND ORTIEG 1870-1939

★ **In 1919, he offered $25,000 to anyone who flew the Atlantic non-stop between Paris and New York.**
★ French-born American restaurateur.
★ The race was won by Charles Lindbergh in 1927.

FRED
OTT 1860-1936

★ **Subject of the first movie close-up; in 1893.**
★ He was Edison's assistant. The shot is of him sneezing and the film was called "Sneeze."

NIKOLAUS AUGUST
OTTO 1832-1891

★ **Inventor of the first effective internal engine; in 1876.**

WILLIAM
OUGHTRED 1575-1660

★ **Introduced the symbol "x" for multiplication; in 1622.**
★ English mathematician who also introduced the abbreviations sin for sine and cos for cosine and invented the slide rule.

RICHARD FELTON
OUTCAULD 1863-1928

★ **Wrote and drew the first classic comic strip in 1896.**
★ It appeared in the *New York World*.

MARY EWING
OUTERBRIDGE

★ **She introduced tennis to the United States; in 1874.**
★ She discovered the game during a visit to Bermuda.

JOHN
OUTRAM

★ **Briton who invented the streetcar in 1775.**
★ The vehicle ran on cast-irons rails and was drawn by two horses.

KARL
PABST

★ **American engineer who designed the Jeep; in 1940.**
★ The name comes from GP (general purpose vehicle).

POTTER
PALMER 1826-1902

★ **First merchant to let customer return or exchange goods.**
★ Owned the Chicago department store that became Marshall Fields; also opened the first fireproof hotel in 1873 in Chicago.

GEORGE NICHOLAS
PAPANICOLAOU 1883-1962

★ **Developer of the Pap smear test for uterine cancer; in 1928.**
★ His work was ignored until 1940.

DENIS
PAPIN 1647-1714

★ **In 1680 developed the first pressure cooker.**
★ He called it the "steam digester."

AMBROSE
PARÉ c.1517-1590

★ **In 1540 devised the first artificial limbs.**
★ He used hinges, cog wheels, levers, etc., to give mobility.
★ French doctor known as father of modern surgery; physician to Henry II, Francis II, Charles IX, Henry III.

MUNGO
PARK 1771-1806

★ **First European to explore the Niger River; in 1795.**

ANDREW BARTON "BANJO" PATERSON 1864-1941

★ **Australian poet who wrote the words for "Waltzing Matilda."**

★ Tune is "Thou Bonnie Wood of Craigielea" by Robert Tannahill.

JOHN HOWARD PAYNE 1791-1852

★ **Wrote the song "Home, Sweet Home" in 1823.**

★ American actor and playwright; also first American to play Hamlet — in Boston in 1809. He was also the American consul to Tunis from 1842 to 1845.

ELIZABETH PALMER PEABODY 1804-1894

★ **Founded first American kindergarten; in Boston in 1860.**

JOHN STITH PEMBERTON

★ **Launched Coca-Cola as a tonic in 1886.**

★ He called it "Esteemed Brain Tonic and Intellectual Beverage."

DOLLY PENTREATH 1685-1777

★ **Widely believed to be the last speaker of Cornish, a Gaelic language.**

★ An English historian studying Cornish translated her last words as "I will not speak English, you ugly black toad!"

GIACOBBO RODRIGUEZ PERIERE 1715-1780

★ **Inventor, in 1749, of sign language for the deaf.**

WILLIAM HENRY
PERKIN 1838-1907

★ **Discovered the first synthetic dye, called mauveine; in 1856.**

FRANCES
PERKINS 1882-1965

★ **She was the first U.S. woman cabinet minister as Secretary of Labor from 1933 to 1945.**

HENRY D.
PERKY

★ **Lawyer who created Shredded Wheat, the first commercial breakfast cereal; in 1893.**

NANCY LING
PERRY 1947-1974

★ **Leader of the Symbionese Liberation Army, the group that kidnapped Patty Hearst.**
★ She was previously a Goldwater supporter.

STEPHEN
PERRY

★ **He patented the rubber band; in 1845.**

LOUIS
PERSINGER 1887-1966

★ **Isaac Stern's violin teacher.**

BETTY JOAN
PERSKE 1924-

★ **Real name of actress Lauren Bacall.**

TRUMAN STRECKFUS PERSONS 1924-1984

★ **Real name of author Truman Capote.**

SUSAN PETERS 1921-1952

★ **Paraplegic actress who appeared in the TV series "Miss Susan" in 1951 playing a wheelchair-bound lawyer.**

PHILIPPE PETIT 1948-

★ **French acrobat who walked a tightrope between two World Trade Center towers; in 1974 in New York City.**
★ He was 1,350 feet over the street. He was immediately arrested.

ALAN PETTIGREW

★ **Threw a haggis 180 feet 10 inches; in 1984 at Loch Lomond.**

JEAN PICARD 1620-1692

★ **The first to compute the size of the earth; in 1671.**

RAOUL PICTET 1846-1929

★ **Swiss chemist and physicist who formulated liquid oxygen.**

OSCAR PIERCE

★ **Texan after whom the Oscar statuette is reputedly named.**
★ The Academy librarian said it looked like her Uncle Oscar.

JANE S. PIERPONT

★ **Wrote the song "Jingle Bells"; in 1857.**

THOMAS PINCKNEY 1750-1828

★ **He ran as vice-president with John Adams in 1796 but Thomas Jefferson was made vice-president due to the electoral college vote.**

GREGORY GOODWIN PINCUS 1903-1967

★ **Headed team that invented the "pill"; in 1954.**

★ The first oral contraceptive pill was marketed in 1961.

LYNDEN PINDLING 1930-

★ **First black prime minister of the Bahamas following its independence from Britain in 1967.**

VICENTE YANEZ PINZON 1460-1524

★ **Spanish navigator who commanded the *Nina* on Columbus's first voyage; in 1492.**

★ Discovered present-day Costa Rica c.1500 and was governor of Puerto Rico in 1505. His brother commanded the *Pinta*.

MARVIN PIPKIN

★ **In 1928, he patented the frosted lightbulb.**

★ It was the first lightbulb that was frosted on the inside, making it last longer.

LEO
PISKER

★ **Has a beer mat collection exceeding 128,000.**
★ The hobby of collecting beer mats is called tegestology.

JAMES L.
PLIMPTON

★ **Former furniture salesman who patented the first workable (four-wheel) roller skate; in 1863.**

ROY J.
PLUNKETT 1910-

★ **American chemist who discovered Teflon; in 1938.**
★ Teflon was a military secret until after World War II.
★ It's the most slippery substance in the world.

LEE
POCKRISS

★ **Co-wrote "Itsy Bitsy Teeny Weeny Yellow Polka Dot Bikini."**

PAUL
POIRET 1879-1944

★ **Fashion designer who freed women from the corset.**
★ Influenced by the Ballet Russe, he introduced harem pants, high waists, etc., in the early 1900s.

CAROL
POLIS

★ **First woman granted a licence to judge boxing; in 1974.**

FREDERICK "FRITZ" DOUGLAS POLLARD 1894-1986

★ **Second black player to be named All-American; in 1915.**

★ William Lewis was the first.

★ Pollard was also first black to coach a pro team (in the 1920s).

STEPHEN J. POPLAWSKI

★ **Patented first blender; in 1922.**

★ It was intended for making malted milk shakes.

WILLIAM SYDNEY PORTER 1862-1910

★ **Real name of short story writer O. Henry.**

★ Convicted for embezzling, he wanted to conceal his identity.

GARY PORTNOY

★ **Co-wrote and recorded the theme to "Cheers."**

★ The other writer is Judy Hart Angelo.

VALDEMAR POULSEN 1869-1942

★ **Danish engineer who built the forerunner of the tape recorder; patented in 1898.**

★ It recorded on piano wire and thus had limited application.

LOUIS PRANG 1824-1909

★ **Boston lithographer and engraver who was the "Father of the American Christmas Card"; produced first one in 1875.**

HONORETTA PRATT
D.1769

★ **Her cremation was the first recorded in Britain; in 1769.**
★ She requested cremation because she believed that decomposition gave off vapours that were harmful to people.
★ Her body was burned in the open grave.

WILLIAM HENRY PRATT
1887-1969

★ **Real name of Boris Karloff.**

PAT PRIEST

★ **First actress to play Marilyn Munster on "The Munsters."**

GABRILLO PRINCIP
1895-1918

★ **Serbian assassin of Archduke Ferdinand and his wife Sophie; in 1914 in Sarajevo.**

JOSHUA PUSEY

★ **American inventor of the match book; in 1892.**
★ His faulty design had the striking surface on the inside of the cover, causing fires.

ISRAEL PUTNAM
1718-1790

★ **Revolutionary general who said, "Don't fire until you see the whites of their eyes" at the Battle of Bunker Hill.**

EUNICE QUEDENS 1912-1990

★ **Real name of Eve Arden (Our Miss Brooks).**

MAE QUESTAL

★ **Provided the voice of Betty Boop (1931 to 1939) as well as Olive Oyl (1933 to 1967).**

HARRIET QUIMBY 1884-1912

★ **First licensed female pilot in the United States.**
★ She was the first woman to fly across the English Channel.
★ She and her passenger died in Boston in the plane she was piloting.

PHINEAS PARKHURST QUIMBY 1802-1866

★ **He was the inspiration for Mary Baker Eddy to found the Christian Science movement.**
★ He performed feats of healing without medication. He was trained as a clockmaker. Eddy was a patient of his in his "mental healing."

MIKE
RACZ

★ **Opened 100 oysters in 2 minutes, 22.17 seconds; in 1987.**

JOSEPH HAYNE
RAINEY 1832-1887

★ **First black congressman; from 1870 to 1879.**
★ This Republican from South Carolina was the son of slaves.

BILL
RAISCH 1905-1984

★ **Actor who played the one-armed man on TV's "The Fugitive."**
★ Lost his arm in World War I; Burt Lancaster's longtime stand-in.

ARMAND JEAN LE BOUTHILLIER DE
RANCÉ 1626-1700

★ **French monk who founded the Trappists.**
★ After a voluptuous life as a courtier-priest, in 1660 underwent a profound change; retired to La Trappe for a life of austerity and devotion. Trappist principles were perpetual prayer, self-denial. Intellectual work was forbidden, only manual labour was allowed.

SUE
RANDALL 1935-1984

★ **Actress who played Miss Randall, Beaver's teacher on "Leave It To Beaver"; from 1959 to 1962.**

JEANETTE
RANKIN 1880-1973

★ **First woman in the House of Representatives.**
★ Republican from Montana whose first term was 1917 to 1919.

VIRGINIA
RAPPE 1896-1921

★ **Woman Fatty Arbuckle was accused of murdering; in 1921.**
★ Arbuckle was never found guilty even after three trials but the scandal ruined his career.

RASMUS CHRISTIAN
RASK 1787-1832

★ **Danish professor who spoke 28 languages.**
★ He compiled and published 235 language dictionaries.

JOHN TATE
RAULSTON 1868-1956

★ **Judge at the 1925 Scopes "Monkey" trial.**

DAVID
RAVEN

★ **Actor who appeared 4,575 times as Major Metcalfe in "The Mousetrap" between 1957 and 1968.**

SHRI N.
RAVI

★ **Balanced on one leg for 34 hours on April 17-18, 1982.**

HORACE
RAWLINS

★ **Won the first U.S. Open Golf Tournament in 1895.**
★ He was 19 at the time and won $150 and a gold medal.

ALEXANDER GILLESPIE
RAYMOND 1909-1956

★ **Newspaper cartoonist who created Flash Gordon; in 1934.**

HENRY JARVIS
RAYMOND 1820-1869

★ **Co-founder of *The New York Times*; in 1851.**

LOUIS
RÉARD 1897-1984

★ **Paris designer of first bikini; in 1946.**
★ The new swim suit was named after the island location (Bikini) of a recent A-bomb test.

JOHANNES
REBMANN 1820-1876

★ **First European to see Mt. Kilimanjaro; in 1849.**
★ He was accompanied by Johann Ludwig Krapf (1810-1881).

ROBERT
RECORDE 1510-1558

★ **English mathematician who was the first to use the symbol = to express equality.**

HEIKKI
REIJONEN

★ **In 1982 designed a 71-foot, 11-inch Cadillac that has 18 wheels, weighs more than 7 tons, has a swimming pool, bar that will hold 20 people, three telephones, a television, and solar deck.**
★ It was built in the United States by Walt Kurozynski.

JESSIE
RENO

★ **Patented escalators; in 1893.**

HIRAM RHODES REVELS 1822-1901

★ **First black U.S. Senator from 1870 to 1871.**
★ He was a Republican from Mississippi.

JEAN RIBAUT 1520-1565

★ **He founded the first French colony in America; in 1562.**
★ It was at present-day Port Royal, South Carolina.

GEORGE FRIEDRICH BERNHARD RIEMANN 1826-1866

★ **Founder of elliptical — non-Euclidean — geometry; in 1854.**
★ Einstein used it to develop his General Theory of Relativity.

CHRIS RIGGIO

★ **Ran 28.5 miles in an egg-and-spoon marathon; in 1979.**
★ It took him 4 hours and 34 minutes.

TERE RIOS

★ **Author of *The Fifteenth Pelican*, the book on which the TV series "The Flying Nun" was based.**

JAMES J. RITTY 1836-1918

★ **Dayton saloon owner who patented the cash register; in 1879.**
★ At first the register was not successful commercially. He sold the patent for $1000 to the company that became National Cash Register.

APOLLOS
RIVOIRE 1735-1818

★ **Huguenot who anglicized his name to...Paul Revere.**

BETTY
ROBBINS

★ **In 1955 was appointed first U.S. woman cantor.**

HENRY MARTYN
ROBERT 1837-1923

★ **The Robert of *Robert's Rules of Order*, first published in 1876.**

XAVIER
ROBERTS

★ **Creator of the Cabbage Patch dolls; in 1977.**
★ They became the doll craze of 1983.

DOANE
ROBINSON

★ **Conceived the idea for Mt. Rushmore; in 1923.**
★ Originally to be Western heroes like Kit Carson, Buffalo Bill Cody.

HENRY CRABB
ROBINSON 1775-1867

★ **British journalist who was first war correspondent; in 1808.**
★ Sent to Spain to cover the peninsular war for the *Times*.

STEPHEN
ROCHE 1959-

★ **First Irishman to win the Tour de France; in 1987.**
★ Also the first English-speaking winner of the Tour of Italy in 1987.

HENRI
ROCHETAIN 1926-

★ **Spent 185 days on a tightrope, including sleeping; in 1973.**
★ The Guinness Book of Records comments that his ability to sleep on the wire left doctors puzzled.

BLOSSOM
ROCK 1896-1978

★ **Played Grandmama on TV's "The Addams Family."**
★ Maiden name was Blossom MacDonald; she was the sister of Jeannette MacDonald. Her married name was Rock.

ANITA LUCIA
RODDICK 1943-

★ **Started the chain of stores, The Body Shop; in 1976.**

JOHN AUGUSTUS
ROEBLING 1806-1869

★ **Designer of the Brooklyn Bridge.**
★ The plans were approved in 1869; Roebling died that same year in June at the site of the proposed bridge.

HENRY
ROMEIKE 1855-1903

★ **Originator of the press-clipping service; in 1883 in Paris.**
★ Opened London branch in 1884 and New York City in 1885.

OLE
RÖMER 1644-1710

★ **Danish astronomer who was the first to measure the speed of light on the basis of astronomical observations; in 1690.**

RICHARD D. ROSEN

★ **Coined the term psychobabble; in 1977.**

JOHN PAUL ROSENBERG

★ **Real name of Werner Erhard, founder of est.**
★ est stands for Erhard Seminars Training, featuring verbal abuse and physical deprivation to transform yourself.

IDA AND WILLIAM ROSENTHAL

★ **Responsible for "sized" bras.**
★ She was a dressmaker who started in the bra business by making two-cup "breast containers." The couple founded Maidenform, and Mr. Rosenthal worked out a system of mass production for the new garments.

CHARLES BREWSTER ROSS

★ **First person in the U.S. ever kidnapped for ransom; in 1874.**
★ He was four years old and was held for $25,000 ransom.

JEAN ROSS 1912-1973

★ **Model for Sally Bowles in *Sally Bowles* and *Goodbye to Berlin*.**

NELLIE TAYLOR ROSS 1876-1977

★ **First woman governor of a state (Wyoming); in 1925.**
★ Also first woman director of U.S. Mint (1933-53).

CLAUDE JOSEPH ROUGET DE LISLE 1760-1836

★ **Composed words and music for "Le Marseillaise"; in 1792.**
★ French army officer and poet.

WILLIAM HENRY ROWE 1884-1945

★ **Inventor of the automatic cigarette vending machine.**

LOUIS RUBENSTEIN 1861-1931

★ **In 1890, he was the first Canadian to win a world figure skating title; in St. Petersburg.**

MARGARET FOGARTY RUDKIN 1897-1967

★ **Founder of Pepperidge Farms Inc.**
★ In 1937 baked whole wheat bread because of her son's allergy. He improved so she made it for other patients via mail-order. She sold the company to Campbell Soup Co. in 1960 for $28 million.

BEARDSLEY RUML 1894-1960

★ **Proposed withholding as a method of collecting income tax.**
★ Passed in 1943 to help servicemen pay taxes on their civilian earnings when earning only minimal wages in the forces.

HAROLD RUSSELL 1914-

★ **Handless Canadian war veteran who won an Academy Award for his performance in "Best Years of Our Lives"; in 1946.**

HANS
SACHS 1494-1576

★ **German meistersinger on whom Wagner based the central character in "Die Meistersinger von Nuremberg"; 1886.**

THOMAS
SAINT

★ **First patent for a sewing machine; London, England, in 1790.**
★ It was used mainly for leather work.

FELIX
SALTEN 1874-1946

★ **Creator of Bambi; in 1926.**

NICOLAS
SAUVAGE

★ **Coachman who opened first taxi business; in 1640 in Paris.**

FRITZ RICHARD
SCHAUDINN 1871-1906

★ **German microbiologist who discovered the syphilis germ in 1905 with Erich Hoffman.**

HARRY
SCHERMAN 1887-1969

★ **Founder of the Book-of-the-Month Club; in 1926.**
★ The club had 40,000 members by the end of the first year.

JOSEPH
SCHILLINGER 1895-1943

★ **George Gershwin's music teacher.**

HEINRICH
SCHLIEMANN 1822-1890

★ **German archaeologist who discovered remains of ancient Troy; in Turkey, in 1871.**
★ Also excavated Mycenae (1876); Ithaca (1878); Boeotia (1881-82).

MAARTEN
SCHMIDT 1929-

★ **Dutch scientist who discovered quasars.**
★ Stands for quasi-stellar radio sources.

ALBERT E.
SCHMUS 1921-

★ **Saw 16,945 films in 32 years.**
★ He was a rater for the Motion Picture Association of America Inc.

OTTO Y.
SCHNERING 1891-1953

★ **First to create brand-name individually wrapped candy bars.**
★ The first bars were Baby Ruth and Butterfingers.

CHRISTIAN FRIEDRICH
SCHONBEIN 1799-1868

★ **German chemist who discovered and named ozone; in 1839.**

SHERWOOD
SCHWARTZ

★ **Creator of "The Brady Bunch."**
★ He also wrote the theme song for "The Brady Bunch" and created "Gilligan's Island."

S

BERTHOLD
SCHWARZ

★ **13th century Franciscan monk who produced the first firearms using gunpowder.**

★ Gunpowder was invented in the 10th century by the Chinese, who never used it for military purposes.

HAZEL
SCOTT 1920-1983

★ **Pianist who was the first black woman to host a network TV series; in 1950.**

JOHANNES DUNS
SCOTUS 1265-1308

★ **The word "dunce" comes from his middle name.**

ELIZABETH COCHRANE
SEAMAN 1867-1922

★ **Went around the world in 72 days to beat the fictional record set in *Around the World in Eighty Days*; from 1889 to 1890.**

★ She was a journalist known as "Nellie Bly" who worked for the New York *World*; pseudonym is from the Stephen Foster song.

EDMUND HAMILTON
SEARS 1810-1876

★ **Wrote words for "It Came Upon a Midnight Clear"; in 1850.**

★ Music was by Richard Storrs Willis.

JAMES
SEHN

★ **Doctor who re-attached John Wayne Bobbitt's penis after his wife Lorena cut it off; in 1993.**

ALEXANDER SELCRAIG 1676-1721

★ **Scottish sailor on whom Defoe based Robinson Crusoe.**

THOMAS ETHOLEN SELFRIDGE D.1908

★ **He was the first airplane fatality; in 1908.**
★ The plane was piloted by Orville Wright.

ISAIAH SELLERS c.1802-1864

★ **Used the pen name "Mark Twain" before Samuel Clemens.**
★ He was a steamboat pilot who used the name for contributions to the New Orleans *Daily Picayune*.

WILLIAM T. SEMPLE

★ **American dentist who patented chewing gum; in 1869.**
★ He didn't do anything with the patent; Thomas Adams, Jr., was the first to start manufacturing it, in 1871.

ALOIS SENEFELDER 1771-1834

★ **Typographer-engraver who invented lithography; in 1796.**
★ Lithography is a process of printing by transfer.

SAMUEL SEWALL 1652-1730

★ **Presiding judge at the Salem witchcraft trials of 1692.**
★ Only Salem judge to ever admit publicly he was in error.

CECIL JAMES SHARP 1859-1924

★ **Founder of the English Folk Dance Society.**

PERCY SHAW

★ **Invented cat's eyes (reflecting road studs).**

★ They enable the motorist to see in dark or foggy conditions. He was a road repairer in Yorkshire who was inspired by seeing a cat's eyes reflecting in the dark.

WASHINGTON WENTWORTH SHEFFIELD

★ **The man who invented the toothpaste tube in 1892.**

★ The first tubes were made of metal.

GRIGORI IVANOVICH SHELEKHOV 1747-1795

★ **He organized the first Russian expedition to Alaska in 1783.**

★ Founded first Russian colony in America on Kodiak Island in 1784.

JAMES SHIELDS 1806-1879

★ **Senator for three different states.**

★ Illinois 1849-1855; Minnesota 1849-1855; Missouri 1879.

CHRISTOPHER LATHAM SHOLES 1819-1890

★ **Inventor of the modern mass-produced typewriter; in 1868.**

★ When he couldn't get financing for his invention, he sold the patent to Remington, the gun manufacturers.

JOHN
SHORE 1662-1752

★ **English trumpeter who invented the tuning fork in 1711.**

JOE
SHUSTER 1914-

★ **Co-creator of Superman; in 1938.**
★ He drew the pictures and Jerry Siegel wrote the words.
★ Shuster didn't register the character as his own and therefore received no royalties.

ANGELO
SICILIANO 1893-1972

★ **Real name of body builder Charles Atlas.**

DAN
SICKLES

★ **In 1859, he was the first to use temporary insanity as a defence in the United States.**
★ He was accused of murdering his wife's lover (son of Francis Scott Key) in a duel; congressman from New York (1857-1861).

CHARLES DWIGHT
SIGSBEE 1845-1923

★ **Commander of the U.S.S. *Maine* which the Spaniards sunk in Havana harbour in 1898.**
★ Catch phrase became "Remember the Maine, Down with Spain."

LOUIS
SILVERS 1889-1954

★ **Composer of "April Showers" for Al Jolson; in 1921.**
★ He also wrote the music for the film "The Jazz Singer" in 1927.

WILLIAM JOSEPH SIMMONS
1880-1945

★ **First imperial wizard of the revived Ku Klux Klan; in 1915.**
★ He was a minister of the Methodist Episcopal Church.

FREDRICK R. SIMMS

★ **Invented the motor car bumper; in 1905.**
★ He based the design on railway engine bumpers.

JAMES YOUNG SIMPSON
1811-1870

★ **Delivered first baby to be born with the aid of anaesthesia; in 1847 in Edinburgh.**
★ Acceptance of anaesthesia in childbirth came when Queen Victoria used it at the birth of Prince Leopold in 1853. He is considered the father of modern gynecology.

TING MING SIONG

★ **Has been best man at more than 465 weddings.**

MARIAN B. SKAGGS
1887-1976

★ **Started the Safeways supermarket chain in the United States.**

NILS NILSSON SKUM
1872-1951

★ **Lapp reindeer herder who became a popular Swedish painter after his retirement.**
★ He took art up at the age of 60.

DOUGLAS BROOKE WHEELTON SLADEN 1856-1947

★ **British writer who compiled the book that became *Who's Who*.**

★ He was editor from 1897 to 1899.

HANS SLOANE 1660-1753

★ **British physician and naturalist whose collection of books formed the basis of the British Museum.**

JOSHUA SLOCUM 1844-1910

★ **First person to sail single-handed around the world; 1895-98.**

★ He set out again in 1909 and was never heard from again.

LEONARD SLYE 1912-

★ **Real name of Roy Rogers.**

WILLIAM SMELLIE 1740-1795

★ **The 28-year-old Scottish scientist and scholar who was the first editor of the *Encyclopedia Britannica*; in 1768.**

★ He was also a printer and set up his own printing business in 1765.

SAMUEL SMILES 1812-1904

★ **Scottish author who coined the phrase "A place for everything, and everything in its place."**

★ He published a book called *Self Help* in 1859.

ROBERT SMIRKE 1781-1867

★ **English architect who built the British Museum (1823-47).**
★ He also built Covent Garden Theatre (1809).

HORTON SMITH 1908-1963

★ **Winner of the first Masters golf tournament; in 1934.**
★ He won by one stroke with a 72-hole score of 284.

JOHN STAFFORD SMITH 1750-1836

★ **British composer of the tune used for "The Star-Spangled Banner."**
★ The tune used was "To Anacreon in Heaven."

LUCIEN B. SMITH

★ **Patented barbed wire in 1867 in Kent, Ohio.**

LUDLOW OGDEN SMITH

★ **Katharine Hepburn's husband.**
★ They separated after three weeks of marriage, but remained lifelong friends.

SAMUEL FRANCIS SMITH 1808-1895

★ **Baptist minister who wrote the words for "My Country 'Tis of Thee" in 1832 to the music of "God Save the King."**
★ Also wrote "Nearer, My God to Thee."

JED
SMITHSON

★ **Invented the ice cream sundae; in 1890.**

★ Storeowner who (when short of ice cream) reduced the portions, but added chocolate sauce or fruit syrup. He did this on Sundays when there were no deliveries (so he called it a Sunday). He changed the spelling due to a complaint that it was sacreligious.

ASCANIO
SOBRERO 1812-1888

★ **Italian chemist who invented nitroglycerin in 1846.**

★ Alfred Nobel demonstrated the practical significance of it.

FREDERICK
SODDY 1877-1956

★ **English physical chemist who coined the word isotope.**

JAN
SOLBERG

★ **Has a collection of 317,800 different beer labels from around the world.**

★ Collecting beer labels is called labology.

GUSTAVE
SONNENBERG 1898-1944

★ **He introduced the "flying tackle" to professional wrestling in 1932.**

CORNELIA
SORABJI 1866-1954

★ **First woman lawyer in India.**

LAZZARO
SPALLANZANI 1729-1799

★ **Italian biologist who undertook the first successful experiments with artificial insemination in 1785.**

★ He also believed and proved that air contained micro-organisms that contaminated food, but people refused to believe him.

DAVE
SPATHAKY

★ **Spun a record 84 plates at once; in 1987 in London.**

PERCY LE BARON
SPENCER

★ **Inventor of the microwave oven in 1945.**

★ A domestic microwave wasn't produced until 1952.

JOHN
SPILSBURY

★ **Englishman who invented jigsaw puzzles in 1760.**

★ The first puzzles were maps glued onto mahogany and then cut into about 50 pieces; he used them to help teach geography.

CARROLL
SPINNEY

★ **Actor who has played Big Bird on "Sesame Street."**

LOUIS
SPOHR 1784-1818

★ **The first to use a baton to conduct an orchestra.**

★ Earlier conductors used rolled-up music sheets, canes, etc.

JOHANNA
SPYRI 1827-1901

★ **Swiss author of *Heidi*.**

FRIEDRICH
STAEDTLER

★ **Founder of the first pencil factory; in Nuremberg in 1660.**

GRACE
STAFFORD

★ **Voice of Woody Woodpecker.**
★ Woody was created by her husband, Walter Lantz. Mel Blanc was the original voice but she replaced him after anonymously entering an audition tape for consideration.

AMOS ALONZO
STAGG 1862-1965

★ **Invented the football tackling dummy.**
★ Also innovator of the huddle, blocking sled, padded goal post, numbered uniforms among other things.

ANDREW TAYLOR
STILL 1828-1917

★ **American founder of osteopathy in 1892.**
★ Coined the term "osteopathy," a combination of the Greek words for bone and suffering.

JOSHUA C.
STODDARD 1814-1902

★ **Invented and patented the steam calliope; in 1855.**
★ It's named after the Greek muse of eloquence and poetry.

LUCY STONE 1818-1893

★ **Reputedly the first married woman to keep her maiden name.**

★ She married Henry Blackwell in 1855. Women who followed her ideas were called Lucy Stoners.

MARVIN CHESTER STONE 1851-1899

★ **Invented the drinking straw in 1888.**

★ It was made of hand-rolled manila paper coated with paraffin.

EMILY JENNINGS STOWE 1831-1903

★ **First woman doctor in Canada.**

★ Got her degree at New York College of Medicine for Women in 1867. She got her licence but didn't practise until 13 years later.

MICHAEL STRANGE 1890-1950

★ **Actress who was the wife of John Barrymore.**

★ Her real name was Blanche Oelricks.

EDWARD STRATEMEYER 1862-1930

★ **The publisher who created Nancy Drew and the Hardy Boys.**

★ Various people wrote these and other series, under names such as Carolyn Keene and Franklin W. Dixon.

CHARLES SHERWOOD STRATTON 1838-1883

★ **Real name of General Tom Thumb.**

★ Was 3'4" tall and joined P. T. Barnum's circus in 1856.

ALMON B.
STROWGER

★ **He is an American undertaker who applied for a patent for the first automatic telephone exchange in 1891.**

ELBRIDGE AMOS
STUART 1856-1944

★ **Founder of the Carnation Company.**
★ He started manufacturing evaporated milk in 1899 in an abandoned hotel in Washington State.

WILLIAM
STURGEON 1783-1850

★ **English physicist who built the first electromagnet in 1825.**

JOHN
SUCKLING 1609-1642

★ **English poet who invented cribbage.**

ROY C.
SULLIVAN D.1983

★ **Survived being struck by lightning seven times between 1942 and 1977.**
★ He was a park ranger; over the years he lost a toe nail and his eyebrows, was seared on a shoulder and legs. Died by suicide.

GIDEON
SUNDBACK 1880-1954

★ **Engineer who perfected the modern zipper; in 1913.**
★ He took the zipper invented by W. Judson and improved on it. The new zippers began to appear in civilian clothing in 1920.

OSCAR GOMER
SWAHN 1847-1927

★ **The world's oldest Olympic medal winner at age 72 years 280 days; in 1920.**

★ Swedish athlete who won a silver medal in the double-shot running deer team event.

JOSEPH WILSON
SWAN 1828-1914

★ **English scientist who shares with Edison the invention of the incandescent electric lamp.**

★ Swan patented his invention in 1878, Edison in 1879.

HENRY
SWEET 1845-1912

★ **G.B. Shaw used him as a model for Henry Higgins in *Pygmalion*, although others have claimed this honour.**

JOE AND BOB
SWITZER

★ **Brothers who invented Day-Glo colours; in 1933.**

FLORENCE MADELEINE "MADGE" CAVE
SYERS 1882-1917

★ **Only woman to enter the 1902 world skating championships.**

★ Came second. Subsequently, a rule was made excluding women. Women's events were introduced in 1906, which she won.

HENRIETTA
SZOLD 1860-1945

★ **Founder of the Jewish women's organization "Hadassah."**

★ Started in 1912, it's the largest women's organization in the U.S.

JUNKO
TABEI 1940-

★ **First woman to reach the top of Mt. Everest; in 1975.**
★ Japanese climber. An avalanche injured 10 of the 15 women who made up the group; only Tabei and a guide reached the top.

RABINDRANATH
TAGOR 1861-1941

★ **Indian poet who was first Asian to win the Nobel Prize for literature; in 1913.**

MARY ANNE
TALBOT 1778-1808

★ **English "Amazon" who served in the English army and navy disguised as a man.**
★ Was a drummer boy in Flanders and a cabin boy in the Navy.

MURRAY
TEICHMAN 1895-

★ **Real name of Arthur Murray, dance teacher.**

VALENTINA VLADIMIROVNA
TERESHKOVA 1937-

★ **Was the first woman to travel in space in Vostok 6; in 1963.**
★ In the three-day flight, she orbited the earth 48 times in 71 hours.

LEWIS MADISON
TERMAN 1877-1956

★ **U.S. psychologist who devised intelligence tests.**
★ Tests are known as "Stanford-Binet" tests.
★ He pioneered the use of the term IQ in 1916.

MARY ELIZA CHURCH TERRELL 1863-1954

★ **First president of the NAACP; from 1896 to 1901.**
★ She was the daughter of slaves and the first black woman to serve on a Washington, D.C., school board.

PAUL H. TERRY 1887-1971

★ **Creator of Mighty Mouse and Heckle and Jeckle.**

FREDERICK WINTHROP THAYER

★ **Invented the catcher's mask; in 1875.**
★ First used in a college game in 1875; professional players adopted it in 1877.

KEITH THIBODEAUX 1950-

★ **Last child to play Little Ricky on "I Love Lucy."**
★ His stage name was Richard Keith.

BARTHÉLEMY THIMMONIER

★ **French tailor who invented the first practical sewing machine; in 1830.**
★ Professional tailors destroyed his factory; they believed the machine threatened their livelihood. Thimmonier died in poverty.

BRANDON THOMAS 1849-1914

★ **English playwright who wrote "Charley's Aunt"; in 1892.**

EVELYN
THOMAS

★ **Involved in the first recorded car accident in the U.S.; in 1896.**
★ She was on a bicycle and suffered a fractured leg in the accident.

NORMAN MATTOON
THOMAS 1884-1968

★ **Ran for president of the U.S. six times between 1928 and 1944.**

BENJAMIN
THOMPSON 1753-1814

★ **Invented the double boiler and drip coffee maker.**

LA MARCUS ADNA
THOMPSON

★ **Built the first roller coaster; in 1885.**
★ It was called the Switchback and was located at Coney Island.

MALVINA CYNTHIA
THOMPSON 1893-1953

★ **Eleanor Roosevelt's secretary from 1932 to 1953.**

JOSEPH JOHN
THOMSON 1856-1940

★ **English physicist who discovered the electron and isotopes.**

NORDAHL (REVEREND)
THORPE

★ **Lutheran minister who married Rock Hudson and Phyllis Gates; in November 1955.**

JOHN S. THURMAN

★ **U.S. inventor of the motor-driven vacuum cleaner; in 1899.**

JOHN HENRY TIMMIS IV

★ **Directed an 85-hour film "Cure for Insomniacs" in 1987.**

GEORGE HOLDEN TINKHAM 1870-1956

★ **Congressman who served 14 terms without making a campaign speech.**

★ He was a Massachusetts Republican who served from 1915 to1943. He was an Isolationist, disapproved of Prohibition, and was an opponent of the New Deal.

MARCUS TULLIUS TIRO

★ **Invented the ampersand (&); about 63 BC.**

★ It was part of the first system of shorthand recorded.

JAMES A. TOBIN 1912-1969

★ **Hit three consecutive home runs in one game; in 1942.**

★ He was a right-handed pitcher with Boston at the time.

CLYDE WILLIAM TOMBAUGH 1906-

★ **Discovered Pluto in 1930.**

★ U.S. astronomer at the Lowell Observatory in Flagstaff. The existence of Pluto was predicted by Percival Lowell in 1915.

AUGUSTUS MONTAGUE
TOPLADY
1740-1778

★ **English minister who wrote words to "Rock of Ages" in 1775.**

TOMAS DE
TORQUEMADA
c.1420-1498

★ **First Grand Inquisitor of the Spanish Inquisition; from 1483.**

★ Spanish Dominican friar who was responsible for the expulsion of Jews from Spain. He was also confessor to King Ferdinand V and Queen Isabella I.

JACK
TORRANCE
1913-1970

★ **Shotput champion who held the world record for 25 years from 1934 to 1959.**

★ He broke the record three times in 1934.

EVANGELISTA
TORRICELLI
1608-1647

★ **Italian physicist who, in 1643, devised the mercury barometer.**

JOHNNY
TORRIO
1882-1957

★ **He led the syndicate that Al Capone took over when Torrio returned to Italy.**

JOHN CRONYN
TOVEY
1885-1971

★ **British admiral who commanded the ship that sank the *Bismarck* in 1941.**

OSWALD
TOWER
1883-1968

★ **Editor of the *Official Basketball Guide*.**

★ Also official interpreter of the rules from 1914 to 1960.

CHARLES HARD
TOWNES
1915-

★ **American physicist who invented the Maser (in 1953).**

★ The Maser is the predecessor of the laser and the microwave equivalent of the laser.

WILLIAM BARRETT
TRAVIS
1809-1836

★ **Commander of the 188 American defenders of the Alamo.**

GEORGE W.
TRENDLE
1885-1972

★ **Creator of "The Green Hornet" and "The Lone Ranger."**

★ "The Lone Ranger" was first heard in 1933 and ran until 1954.

RICHARD
TREVITHICK
1771-1833

★ **Developed the first practical steam locomotive in 1801.**

★ English engineer and mechanic; also responsible for the first steam engine to run on rails in 1804.

TSAI-LUN
c.50-c.118

★ **Chinese court official who invented paper c.105.**

★ Although Egyptians had made papyrus from grass, he broke plants down into fibres by beating them and making them into a sheet of paper.

OSCAR MICHEL
TSCHIRKY 1866-1950

★ **Credited with the creation of the Waldorf salad.**
★ Maitre d' of the Waldorf Hotel from 1893 to 1943.

EIJI
TSUBURUYA

★ **Created special effects in "Godzilla vs. the Smog Monster."**
★ He also designed the title character in "Godzilla" in 1954.

YOSHIAKI
TSUTSUMI

★ **World's richest man in 1988 according to *Forbes* magazine.**
★ He made his fortune in real estate and transport companies. His assets in 1988 were $18,900 million.

LAURENCE
TUREAUD 1952-

★ **Real name of Mr. T.**
★ In his role in "The A-Team," he wore 35 pounds of gold jewellery.

FANNIE
TURNER 1903-

★ **She took 104 attempts to pass her written driver's licence in the United States.**

JOHN
TYNDALL 1820-1893

★ **Irish physicist who discovered why the sky is blue; in 1870.**
★ "Tyndall effect" states that the "scattering of light by small particles of water" causes the sky to be blue.

NICHOLAS
UDALL 1505-1556

★ **Wrote first English comedy – "Ralph Roister Doister" in 1550.**

ALBERT
UDERZO

RENÉ
GOSCINNY

★ **Creators of the Asterix cartoon character.**
★ The cartoon was first published in 1959 and the character has gone on to star in films, radio programs, and computer games.

BERRIEN KINNARD "RED"
UPSHAW

★ **Model for Rhett Butler in *Gone With The Wind*.**
★ Margaret Mitchell's first husband.

HEZEKIAH
USHER

★ **Opened first store in U.S. to sell books; in Boston in 1639.**

CATHY
USHLER

★ **In 1987 made a gum wrapper chain — 5,967 feet long — longest that had been completed to that time.**

ARCHBISHOP JAMES
USSHER 1581-1656

★ **Claimed in 1654 that the earth had been created on October 26, 4004 BC at 9 a.m.**
★ Ussher (whose name sometimes appears as Usher) was an Irish priest and archbishop. The figure appeared in the margin of the Authorized Version of the Bible until the 19th century.

THEODORE NEWTON VAIL 1845-1920

★ **Founder of Western Union Telegraph Co. (1881) and president of AT&T.**

★ Started as telegrapher. Was instrumental in laying first transcontinental telephone cable in 1915.

WLADZUI VALENTINO 1919-1987

★ **Real name of Liberace.**

THEOPHILUS VAN KANNEL

★ **Inventor of the revolving door — patented in 1888.**

★ Used in skyscrapers where the air pressure outside and suction from elevators inside made convential doors difficult to open.

LEUDOLPH VAN CEULEN 1540-1610

★ **Spent much of his life calculating pi to 35 decimal places.**

★ Dutch mathematician; the number is called Leudolph's number and its value is inscribed on his tombstone in Leiden.

JEAN BAPTISTE VAN HELMONT 1577-1644

★ **Belgium chemist and scientist who recognized existence of different gases, coined the word gas from the Greek *chaos*.**

COENRAD VAN HOUTEN

★ **In 1828 obtained cocoa by extracting cocoa butter from the crushed cocoa beans.**

PIETER
VAN LOGGERENBERG

★ **Played an accordion for 85 hours non-stop, a world record.**

JOHN
VANBRUGH 1664-1726

★ **English playwright who turned to architecture and designed Castle Howard (1702) and Blenheim Palace (1705).**

JEAN
VANDERPYL

★ **She did the voices of Wilma and Pebbles Flintstone.**
★ She was also Ogee on "Magilla Gorilla."

HARRY
VARDON 1870-1937

★ **Six-time winner of the British Open between 1896 and 1914.**

THORSTEIN BUNDE
VEBLEN 1857-1929

★ **American economist who coined the term "conspicuous consumption."**
★ He was one of the first to apply psychology to the study of business and economics.

PIERRE
VERDUN

★ **Inventor of the Cuisinart; in 1963 in France.**
★ At first it was sold only to professional chefs, under the name Robot-Coupe. It was introduced to North America by Carl Sontheimer in 1973.

EDWARD
VERNON 1684-1757

★ **Washington named Mt. Vernon after him.**

ALVIN
VERRETTE

★ **Opened a drive-in funeral parlour; in Louisiana in 1970s.**

★ The corpse was displayed behind a glass window near the driveway at the side of the building. A register was set on a podium so visitors could sign.

ANDREA DEL
VERROCCHIO 1435-1488

★ **Italian sculptor who taught Leonardo da Vinci.**

FRANÇOIS
VIÈTE 1540-1603

★ **First to use letters of the alphabet to denote both known and unknown quantities in algebra.**

★ French mathematician who invented algebra in its modern form, in late 16th century; used symbols similar to the ones used today.

RAINER
VIKSTRÖM

★ **Shook the hands of 19,592 people (with no repeats) in eight hours in 1988. The event took place in Turku, Finland.**

AUGUST HEINRICH HOFFMANN
VON FALLERSLEBEN 1798-1874

★ **Wrote poem "Deutschland, Deutschland uber alles"; in 1841.**

★ It was used as a German national hymn from 1922.

CHARLES FREDERICK VON GERHARDT 1816-1856

★ **French chemist who was first to synthesize aspirin; in 1853.**

★ He wasn't particularly interested in its practical uses. It was a young German chemist, Felix Hoffman, who in 1893 re-discovered its pain-easing properties in a search to relieve his father's arthritis.

BERTHA KINSKY VON SUTTNER 1843-1914

★ **Suggested idea of a peace prize to Nobel; in 1885.**

★ Nobel's housekeeper and secretary. After she left his employ, she devoted herself to anti-war campaigns, writing books, and giving lectures; she was the first woman to win the Nobel Prize for Peace, in 1905.

SERGE VORONOV 1866-1951

★ **Russian doctor who pioneered "rejuvenation" of old men using monkey glands.**

★ Director of experimental surgery at the College de France.

CARL POTTER VOSS 1907-

★ **First rookie of the year in the NHL; after the 1932-33 season.**

★ He played for the Detroit Red Wings.

★ The Calder Trophy is now awarded to the rookie of the year.

JOHANN
WAALER

★ **Norwegian inventor who invented the paper clip; in 1900.**

CHARLES C.
WAITE

★ **First player to wear a baseball glove; in 1875.**
★ He also developed it. It was an unpadded glove.

SELMAN ABRAHAM
WAKSMAN 1888-1973

★ **American scientist who originated the term "antibiotics."**
★ Also discovered streptomycin; in 1943.

LILLIAN D.
WALD 1867-1940

★ **Social worker who pioneered public health nursing in U.S.**
★ Also started first city school nurse service in 1902 in New York.

JANET
WALDO

★ **Voice of Judy Jetson.**

MARTIN
WALDSEEMULLER c.1480-c.1521

★ **German mapmaker who named the New World America, after Amerigo Vespucci; in 1507.**

NATHANIEL B.
WALES 1883-1974

★ **American who designed the Kelvinator fridge in 1918.**

JOHN
WALKER 1781-1859

★ **English druggist who invented the friction match in 1827.**

MAGGIE LENA
WALKER

★ **First black female bank president in U.S.; in 1903.**
★ She worked for the St. Luke Penny Savings Bank in Virginia.

MARY EDWARDS
WALKER 1832-1919

★ **Only female winner of the U.S. Medal of Honor; in 1865.**
★ She was a surgeon during the Civil War and was appointed the official army surgeon in 1863.
★ She was arrested several times for wearing trousers on the street.

SARA BREEDLOVE
WALKER 1867-1919

★ **She was the first woman millionaire in the United States.**
★ She was a black who made her fortune in hair care products; her first product was a hair straightener.

ALFRED RUSSELL
WALLACE 1823-1913

★ **British naturalist who developed theory of evolution concurrently with Darwin.**

DE WITT
WALLACE 1899-1981

★ **Publisher who started *Reader's Digest*; in 1922.**
★ Lila Acheson started it with him.

LEWIS WALLACE 1827-1905

★ **Author of *Ben Hur;* in 1880.**

★ He was the governor of New Mexico territory at the time.

AUGUSTUS DÉSIRÉ WALLER 1856-1922

★ **He performed the first electrocardiogram on a human; in 1887 at London University.**

FREDERIC WALLER 1886-1954

★ **Inventor of Cinerama process.**

★ It debuted in 1952 with "This Is Cinerama," a travelogue.

FREDERICK WALTON

★ **Englishman who created linoleum in 1863.**

ARCH WARD 1896-1955

★ **Sports editor for the *Chicago Tribune* who originated the idea of all-star baseball and football games.**

★ The first all-star game was at the Chicago Centennial Exposition of Progress in 1933. It has become an annual event.

JACK WARHOP

★ **New York Yankees pitcher off whom Babe Ruth hit his first major league home run on May 6, 1915.**

CORNELIUS
WARMERDAM 1915-

★ **He was the first person to pole vault 15 feet; in 1940.**
★ American who held the world record seven times.

EZRA J.
WARNER

★ **Patented first can opener in 1858.**
★ Patented almost 50 years after canned food was invented.

SIMON WARONKER — **AL BENNETT** — **TED KEEP**

★ **Alvin and the Chipmunks were named after them.**
★ All three worked for Liberty Records, the Chipmunks' label.

JOSEPH
WARREN 1741-1775

★ **Revolutionary general who sent Paul Revere and William Dawes on their famous ride.**

GUY
WEADICK 1885-1953

★ **Originated the idea for the Calgary Stampede; first held 1912.**

KEN
WEATHERWAX

★ **Actor who played Pugsley on TV's "The Addams Family."**

RUDD
WEATHERWAX

★ **He was the owner and trainer of "Lassie."**

MATTHEW
WEBB 1848-1883

★ **First to swim the English Channel; in 1875.**

★ It took him 21 hours and 45 minutes to go from Dover to Calais. He drowned trying to swim the Niagara rapids.

RALPH
WEDGWOOD

★ **Patented carbon paper in 1806.**

HARRY D.
WEED

★ **Invented snow chains for car tires; in 1904 in New York.**

ALFRED LOTHAR
WEGENER 1880-1930

★ **Geographer who coined the term continental drift; in 1915.**

EUGENE
WEIDMANN D.1939

★ **Last person to be publicly guillotined in France.**

JACK
WEINSTOCK 1907-1969

★ **Urologist who was co-author of musical "How To Succeed in Business Without Really Trying."**

★ He did it with Abe Burrows and Willie Gilbert.

EHRICH
WEISS 1874-1926

★ **Real name of Harry Houdini.**

K. ST. VINCENT WELCH

★ **First doctor in the Australian Flying Doctor Service; in 1928.**

★ The first year he flew 32,000 km in 50 flights, visiting 255 patients.

HORACE WELLS 1815-1845

★ **First to use laughing gas as anaesthetic for dentistry; in 1844.**

★ American dentist; used it on himself to extract a tooth.

ELLA WENDEL D.1931

★ **She left £15 million to her poodle Toby.**

JOHN ARCHIBALD WHEELER

★ **Coined the term "black hole"; in 1967.**

★ The term describes a star that has collapsed completely.

ERIC WHELPTON 1894-1981

★ **Dorothy Sayers used him as her model for Peter Wimsey.**

★ She was in love with this schoolteacher and travel writer but he did not return her feelings.

WILLIAM ALLEN WHITE 1868-1944

★ **American writer and journalist who coined the phrase "All dressed up with nowhere to go"; in 1916.**

★ He was referring to the Progressive Party in the U.S. after Theodore Roosevelt retired from the campaign.

ROBERT
WHITEHEAD 1823-1905

★ **English inventor of the self-propelled torpedo (1866).**

CASPAR
WHITNEY

★ **Sportswriter for *Harper's Weekly* who began the tradition of picking All-Americans in college football.**

FRANK
WHITTLE 1907-

★ **English engineer, inventor of the modern jet engine in 1930.**

JOSEPH (SIR)
WHITWORTH 1803-1887

★ **The English mechanical engineer who standardized screw threads.**

EDWARD
WHYMPER 1840-1911

★ **He was the first to climb the Matterhorn (1865).**

ROBERT C.
WIAN, JR.

★ **Invented the double-decker hamburger; in 1936 in California.**
★ He called it a Big Boy.

CARL ERIC
WICKMAN 1887-1954

★ **Co-founder of the Greyhound Bus Line; in 1930.**
★ He was president from 1930 to 1946, and chairman of the board from 1946 to 1951.

JOHANN
WIDMANN

★ **First to use plus and minus signs; in 1489.**

KATE DOUGLAS
WIGGIN 1856-1923

★ **American who wrote *Rebecca of Sunnybrook Farm* in 1903.**

ELLA WHEELER
WILCOX 1855-1919

★ **American poet who wrote "Laugh and the world laughs with you; Weep and you weep alone" in her poem "Solitude."**

JAMES MILLER
WILLIAMS

★ **Canadian who drilled the world's first oil well; in June 1858.**
★ It was located in Enniskillen Township, Ontario, Canada.

WALTER
WILLIAMS 1842-1959

★ **Last surviving Civil War veteran, who died at age 117.**

CLOUGH
WILLIAMS-ELLIS 1883-1978

★ **British architect who designed the Welsh town of Portmeirion that was used as the set for "The Prisoner."**

GEORGE
WILLIG

★ **Scaled World Trade Center in 1977.**

KEMMONS
WILSON 1913-

★ **Founder of Holiday Inn; in 1952.**
★ The first Holiday Inn motel was in Memphis, Tennessee.

SAMUEL
WILSON 1766-1854

★ **American meat packer, officially recognized by the Kennedy administration as the progenitor of "Uncle Sam."**

WALTER CLOMPTON
WINGFIELD 1833-1912

★ **In 1874, patented a game that became known as lawn tennis.**

SEPTIMUS
WINNER 1827-1902

★ **Wrote "Listen To the Mockingbird" and "Oh Where, Oh Where, Has My Little Dog Gone?"**

WILLIAM
WIRT 1772-1834

★ **Ran for president in 1832 for the first third party in the United States; it was called the Anti-Masonic Party.**

NIKLAUS
WIRTH

★ **Swiss who invented the computer language PASCAL; in 1970.**

WILLIAM
WITHERING 1741-1799

★ **English physician who discovered digitalis in 1775.**

LOTHROP
WITHINGTON, JR.

★ **He was a Harvard student who started the live goldfish-eating craze in 1939.**

LEONARD
WOOD 1860-1927

★ **U.S. Army general who helped organize the Rough Riders in 1898 and friend of Teddy Roosevelt.**

VICTORIA CLAFLIN
WOODHULL 1838-1927

★ **First female presidential nominee in U.S.; in 1872.**
★ She was named by the National Radical Reformers.

WILLIAM E.
WOODWARD 1875-1950

★ **American novelist who created the word "debunk."**

HENRY CLAY
WORK 1832-1884

★ **Wrote the temperance song "Father, dear father, come home with me now..."; in 1864.**

CLEMENT
WRAGGE

★ **First to name tropical storms.**
★ Australian meteorologist who at the turn of the century gave storms names of women and politicians; anticyclones were named after people he liked and named low-pressure systems after people he didn't like.

FRANK **ROY**

WRIGHT **ALLEN**

★ **Their root beer stand was the start of the A&W fast-food empire in 1923.**

GEORGE

WRIGHT

★ **In 1869 he was the top earning baseball player of the first salaried baseball team; he earned $1,400.**

★ He was captain and shortstop of the Cincinatti Red Stockings. Brother Harry was manager and centre field and earned $1,200.

JAMES

WRIGHT

★ **Engineer who invented Silly Putty—by mistake while experimenting with synthetic rubber in 1945.**

ARTHUR

WYNNE

★ **Journalist who created the first crossword puzzle.**

★ It appeared in the New York *World* on December 12, 1913.

PETER

WYSHNER

★ **Only one-armed outfielder in major league baseball.**

★ Played for St. Louis Browns in 1945 under the name of Pete Gray.

MAX
YASGUR

★ **Dairy farmer on whose farm Woodstock was held; in 1969.**
★ The farm was 600 acres; the festival temporarily made it the third largest city in New York state, with 250,000 people.

SARAH AND ADELAIDE
YATES

★ **These sisters married Siamese twins Chang and Eng Bunker in 1843.**

YOSHIOKA
YAYOI 1871-1959

★ **First Japanese woman doctor; in 1892.**

ALEXANDRE EMILE JOHN
YERSIN 1863-1943

★ **Discovered plague bacillus in 1894 and prepared antiserum.**
★ Also introduced rubber tree into Indochina.

VINCENT
YOUMANS 1898-1946

★ **Wrote "Tea for Two," "The Carioca," and many others.**

FELIX
YOUSSOUPOFF 1886-1967

★ **Russian responsible for the assassination of Rasputin in 1916.**

VICTOR SEN
YUNG 1915-

★ **Actor who played cook Hop Sing on "Bonanza."**

Z

EMANUEL
ZACCHINI

★ **Holds the human cannonball record: he was shot 175 feet in 1940.**

JONATHAN THOMAS "TOM" W.
ZACHARY 1896-1969

★ **Pitched Babe Ruth's 60th homer to him in 1927.**

LAZARUS LUDWIG
ZAMENHOF 1859-1917

★ **Created the international language of Esperanto in 1887.**

★ Polish oculist and philologist; his aim was to promote peace and understanding. Esperanto means "one who hopes."

GIUSEPPE
ZANGARA 1900-1933

★ **Italian anarchist who tried to murder F.D. Roosevelt; in 1933.**

ISRAEL
ZANGWILL 1864-1926

★ **English writer who originated the phrase "melting pot" in its modern sense of mixing many cultures to make one.**

EMIL
ZATOPEK 1922-

★ **Czech soldier who won the 5,000 m, 10,000 m, and the marathon, setting world records for each in 1952 Olympics.**

MARGARETHA GEERTRUIDA
ZELLE 1876-1917

★ **Mata Hari's real name.**

Z

JOHN PETER
ZENGER 1697-1746

★ **New York printer and editor whose libel trial established freedom of the press in the United States; in 1735.**

JOHN
ZIZKA D.1424

★ **Page to King Wenceslaus.**
★ Became Czech soldier who anticipated modern tank warfare by use of artillery on armoured wagons.

PAUL
ZOLLE

★ **Developed the first external pacemaker.**

ALEXANDRA
ZUCK 1942-

★ **Real name of Sandra Dee.**

ROBERT CARL
ZUPPKE 1879-1957

★ **Football coach who "invented" the huddle.**

VLADIMIR KOSMA
ZWORKYIN 1889-1982

★ **The first video camera was developed as a result of his work.**
★ Considered the father of TV; pioneer in development of electron microscope. Invented TV transmitter in 1923; kinescope (TV receiver) in 1924; first practical TV system in 1938. He also invented the sniperscope and snooperscope.

★ ★ ★ BLUFFLE ★ ★ ★

NAME

BIOGRAPHY

PLAYER	VOTE					

NAME

BIOGRAPHY

PLAYER	VOTE					

NAME

BIOGRAPHY

PLAYER	VOTE					

NAME

BIOGRAPHY

PLAYER	VOTE					

NAME

BIOGRAPHY

PLAYER	VOTE					

NAME

BIOGRAPHY

PLAYER	VOTE					

★ ★ ★ BLUFFLE ★ ★ ★

NAME

BIOGRAPHY

PLAYER VOTE

NAME

BIOGRAPHY

PLAYER VOTE

NAME

BIOGRAPHY

PLAYER VOTE

NAME

BIOGRAPHY

PLAYER VOTE

NAME

BIOGRAPHY

PLAYER VOTE

NAME

BIOGRAPHY

PLAYER VOTE

★ ★ ★ BLUFFLE ★ ★ ★

NAME

BIOGRAPHY

PLAYER VOTE

NAME

BIOGRAPHY

PLAYER VOTE

NAME

BIOGRAPHY

PLAYER VOTE

NAME

BIOGRAPHY

PLAYER VOTE

NAME

BIOGRAPHY

PLAYER VOTE

NAME

BIOGRAPHY

PLAYER VOTE

★ ★ ★ BLUFFLE ★ ★ ★

NAME

BIOGRAPHY

PLAYER	VOTE					

NAME

BIOGRAPHY

PLAYER	VOTE					

NAME

BIOGRAPHY

PLAYER	VOTE					

NAME

BIOGRAPHY

PLAYER	VOTE					

NAME

BIOGRAPHY

PLAYER	VOTE					

NAME

BIOGRAPHY

PLAYER	VOTE					

★ ★ ★ BLUFFLE ★ ★ ★

NAME

BIOGRAPHY

PLAYER	VOTE					

NAME

BIOGRAPHY

PLAYER	VOTE					

NAME

BIOGRAPHY

PLAYER	VOTE					

NAME

BIOGRAPHY

PLAYER	VOTE					

NAME

BIOGRAPHY

PLAYER	VOTE					

NAME

BIOGRAPHY

PLAYER	VOTE					

★ ★ ★ BLUFFLE ★ ★ ★

NAME

BIOGRAPHY

PLAYER	VOTE					

NAME

BIOGRAPHY

PLAYER	VOTE					

NAME

BIOGRAPHY

PLAYER	VOTE					

NAME

BIOGRAPHY

PLAYER	VOTE					

NAME

BIOGRAPHY

PLAYER	VOTE					

NAME

BIOGRAPHY

PLAYER	VOTE					

BLUFFLE

NAME

BIOGRAPHY

PLAYER VOTE

NAME

BIOGRAPHY

PLAYER VOTE

NAME

BIOGRAPHY

PLAYER VOTE

NAME

BIOGRAPHY

PLAYER VOTE

NAME

BIOGRAPHY

PLAYER VOTE

NAME

BIOGRAPHY

PLAYER VOTE

★ ★ ★ BLUFFLE ★ ★ ★

NAME

BIOGRAPHY

PLAYER	VOTE					

NAME

BIOGRAPHY

PLAYER	VOTE					

NAME

BIOGRAPHY

PLAYER	VOTE					

NAME

BIOGRAPHY

PLAYER	VOTE					

NAME

BIOGRAPHY

PLAYER	VOTE					

NAME

BIOGRAPHY

PLAYER	VOTE					

★ ★ ★ BLUFFLE ★ ★ ★

NAME

BIOGRAPHY

PLAYER VOTE

NAME

BIOGRAPHY

PLAYER VOTE

NAME

BIOGRAPHY

PLAYER VOTE

NAME

BIOGRAPHY

PLAYER VOTE

NAME

BIOGRAPHY

PLAYER VOTE

NAME

BIOGRAPHY

PLAYER VOTE

★ ★ ★ BLUFFLE ★ ★ ★

NAME

BIOGRAPHY

PLAYER **VOTE**

NAME

BIOGRAPHY

PLAYER **VOTE**

NAME

BIOGRAPHY

PLAYER **VOTE**

NAME

BIOGRAPHY

PLAYER **VOTE**

NAME

BIOGRAPHY

PLAYER **VOTE**

NAME

BIOGRAPHY

PLAYER **VOTE**

★ ★ ★ BLUFFLE ★ ★ ★

NAME

BIOGRAPHY

PLAYER	VOTE					

NAME

BIOGRAPHY

PLAYER	VOTE					

NAME

BIOGRAPHY

PLAYER	VOTE					

NAME

BIOGRAPHY

PLAYER	VOTE					

NAME

BIOGRAPHY

PLAYER	VOTE					

NAME

BIOGRAPHY

PLAYER	VOTE					

★ ★ ★ BLUFFLE ★ ★ ★

NAME

BIOGRAPHY

PLAYER	VOTE					

NAME

BIOGRAPHY

PLAYER	VOTE					

NAME

BIOGRAPHY

PLAYER	VOTE					

NAME

BIOGRAPHY

PLAYER	VOTE					

NAME

BIOGRAPHY

PLAYER	VOTE					

NAME

BIOGRAPHY

PLAYER	VOTE					

★ ★ ★ BLUFFLE ★ ★ ★

NAME

BIOGRAPHY

PLAYER	VOTE					

NAME

BIOGRAPHY

PLAYER	VOTE					

NAME

BIOGRAPHY

PLAYER	VOTE					

NAME

BIOGRAPHY

PLAYER	VOTE					

NAME

BIOGRAPHY

PLAYER	VOTE					

NAME

BIOGRAPHY

PLAYER	VOTE					

★ ★ ★ BLUFFLE ★ ★ ★

NAME

BIOGRAPHY

PLAYER	VOTE					

NAME

BIOGRAPHY

PLAYER	VOTE					

NAME

BIOGRAPHY

PLAYER	VOTE					

NAME

BIOGRAPHY

PLAYER	VOTE					

NAME

BIOGRAPHY

PLAYER	VOTE					

NAME

BIOGRAPHY

PLAYER	VOTE					

★ ★ ★ BLUFFLE ★ ★ ★

NAME

BIOGRAPHY

PLAYER	VOTE					

NAME

BIOGRAPHY

PLAYER	VOTE					

NAME

BIOGRAPHY

PLAYER	VOTE					

NAME

BIOGRAPHY

PLAYER	VOTE					

NAME

BIOGRAPHY

PLAYER	VOTE					

NAME

BIOGRAPHY

PLAYER	VOTE					

★ ★ ★ BLUFFLE ★ ★ ★

NAME

BIOGRAPHY

PLAYER **VOTE**

NAME

BIOGRAPHY

PLAYER **VOTE**

NAME

BIOGRAPHY

PLAYER **VOTE**

NAME

BIOGRAPHY

PLAYER **VOTE**

NAME

BIOGRAPHY

PLAYER **VOTE**

NAME

BIOGRAPHY

PLAYER **VOTE**

★ ★ ★ BLUFFLE ★ ★ ★

NAME

BIOGRAPHY

PLAYER VOTE

NAME

BIOGRAPHY

PLAYER VOTE

NAME

BIOGRAPHY

PLAYER VOTE

NAME

BIOGRAPHY

PLAYER VOTE

NAME

BIOGRAPHY

PLAYER VOTE

NAME

BIOGRAPHY

PLAYER VOTE

BLUFFLE

NAME

BIOGRAPHY

PLAYER VOTE

NAME

BIOGRAPHY

PLAYER VOTE

NAME

BIOGRAPHY

PLAYER VOTE

NAME

BIOGRAPHY

PLAYER VOTE

NAME

BIOGRAPHY

PLAYER VOTE

NAME

BIOGRAPHY

PLAYER VOTE

★ ★ ★ BLUFFLE ★ ★ ★

NAME

BIOGRAPHY

PLAYER VOTE

NAME

BIOGRAPHY

PLAYER VOTE

NAME

BIOGRAPHY

PLAYER VOTE

NAME

BIOGRAPHY

PLAYER VOTE

NAME

BIOGRAPHY

PLAYER VOTE

NAME

BIOGRAPHY

PLAYER VOTE

★ ★ ★ BLUFFLE ★ ★ ★

NAME

BIOGRAPHY

PLAYER	VOTE					

NAME

BIOGRAPHY

PLAYER	VOTE					

NAME

BIOGRAPHY

PLAYER	VOTE					

NAME

BIOGRAPHY

PLAYER	VOTE					

NAME

BIOGRAPHY

PLAYER	VOTE					

NAME

BIOGRAPHY

PLAYER	VOTE					

★ ★ ★ BLUFFLE ★ ★ ★

NAME

BIOGRAPHY

PLAYER VOTE

NAME

BIOGRAPHY

PLAYER VOTE

NAME

BIOGRAPHY

PLAYER VOTE

NAME

BIOGRAPHY

PLAYER VOTE

NAME

BIOGRAPHY

PLAYER VOTE

NAME

BIOGRAPHY

PLAYER VOTE

★ ★ ★ BLUFFLE ★ ★ ★

NAME

BIOGRAPHY

PLAYER VOTE

NAME

BIOGRAPHY

PLAYER VOTE

NAME

BIOGRAPHY

PLAYER VOTE

NAME

BIOGRAPHY

PLAYER VOTE

NAME

BIOGRAPHY

PLAYER VOTE

NAME

BIOGRAPHY

PLAYER VOTE

BLUFFLE

NAME

BIOGRAPHY

PLAYER VOTE

NAME

BIOGRAPHY

PLAYER VOTE

NAME

BIOGRAPHY

PLAYER VOTE

NAME

BIOGRAPHY

PLAYER VOTE

NAME

BIOGRAPHY

PLAYER VOTE

NAME

BIOGRAPHY

PLAYER VOTE

★ ★ ★ BLUFFLE ★ ★ ★

NAME

BIOGRAPHY

PLAYER VOTE

NAME

BIOGRAPHY

PLAYER VOTE

NAME

BIOGRAPHY

PLAYER VOTE

NAME

BIOGRAPHY

PLAYER VOTE

NAME

BIOGRAPHY

PLAYER VOTE

NAME

BIOGRAPHY

PLAYER VOTE

★ ★ ★ BLUFFLE ★ ★ ★

NAME						
BIOGRAPHY						
PLAYER	**VOTE**					

NAME						
BIOGRAPHY						
PLAYER	**VOTE**					

NAME						
BIOGRAPHY						
PLAYER	**VOTE**					

NAME						
BIOGRAPHY						
PLAYER	**VOTE**					

NAME						
BIOGRAPHY						
PLAYER	**VOTE**					

NAME						
BIOGRAPHY						
PLAYER	**VOTE**					

★ ★ ★ BLUFFLE ★ ★ ★

NAME

BIOGRAPHY

PLAYER **VOTE**

NAME

BIOGRAPHY

PLAYER **VOTE**

NAME

BIOGRAPHY

PLAYER **VOTE**

NAME

BIOGRAPHY

PLAYER **VOTE**

NAME

BIOGRAPHY

PLAYER **VOTE**

NAME

BIOGRAPHY

PLAYER **VOTE**

★ ★ ★ BLUFFLE ★ ★ ★

NAME

BIOGRAPHY

PLAYER	VOTE					

NAME

BIOGRAPHY

PLAYER	VOTE					

NAME

BIOGRAPHY

PLAYER	VOTE					

NAME

BIOGRAPHY

PLAYER	VOTE					

NAME

BIOGRAPHY

PLAYER	VOTE					

NAME

BIOGRAPHY

PLAYER	VOTE					

★ ★ ★ BLUFFLE ★ ★ ★

NAME

BIOGRAPHY

PLAYER	VOTE					

NAME

BIOGRAPHY

PLAYER	VOTE					

NAME

BIOGRAPHY

PLAYER	VOTE					

NAME

BIOGRAPHY

PLAYER	VOTE					

NAME

BIOGRAPHY

PLAYER	VOTE					

NAME

BIOGRAPHY

PLAYER	VOTE					

★ ★ ★ BLUFFLE ★ ★ ★

NAME

BIOGRAPHY

PLAYER VOTE

NAME

BIOGRAPHY

PLAYER VOTE

NAME

BIOGRAPHY

PLAYER VOTE

NAME

BIOGRAPHY

PLAYER VOTE

NAME

BIOGRAPHY

PLAYER VOTE

NAME

BIOGRAPHY

PLAYER VOTE

★ ★ ★ BLUFFLE ★ ★ ★

NAME

BIOGRAPHY

PLAYER	VOTE					

NAME

BIOGRAPHY

PLAYER	VOTE					

NAME

BIOGRAPHY

PLAYER	VOTE					

NAME

BIOGRAPHY

PLAYER	VOTE					

NAME

BIOGRAPHY

PLAYER	VOTE					

NAME

BIOGRAPHY

PLAYER	VOTE					

BLUFFLE

NAME

BIOGRAPHY

PLAYER	VOTE					

NAME

BIOGRAPHY

PLAYER	VOTE					

NAME

BIOGRAPHY

PLAYER	VOTE					

NAME

BIOGRAPHY

PLAYER	VOTE					

NAME

BIOGRAPHY

PLAYER	VOTE					

NAME

BIOGRAPHY

PLAYER	VOTE					

★ ★ ★ BLUFFLE ★ ★ ★

NAME

BIOGRAPHY

PLAYER	VOTE					

NAME

BIOGRAPHY

PLAYER	VOTE					

NAME

BIOGRAPHY

PLAYER	VOTE					

NAME

BIOGRAPHY

PLAYER	VOTE					

NAME

BIOGRAPHY

PLAYER	VOTE					

NAME

BIOGRAPHY

PLAYER	VOTE					